# Ginn Mathematics 5

## TEXTBOOK 2

GINN

# Multiplication of 2-digit numbers.

Some of these questions can be answered by multiplying.

Some can't!

Look at each one. Can it be solved using multiplying? Write yes or no.

If it can be answered by multiplying, write the multiplication and find the answer.

31 children and 3 teachers went on a farm visit. They took a pair of wellies each. How many wellies were there altogether?

yes or no?  yes

$$\begin{array}{r} 34 \\ \times\ 2 \\ \hline 68 \end{array}$$

1   56 children need tickets for a play. The teacher has 4 tickets. How many more do they need?

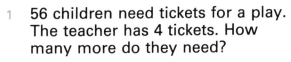

yes or no?

2   11 children were painting. They had 8 paint sticks each. How many paint sticks had to be collected up afterwards?

yes or no?

3   Sanjit's auntie made 12 buns for Sanjit and his 2 sisters, How many could they have each?

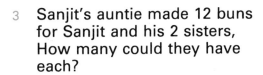

yes or no?

4   Sam, Jo and Babs are triplets. They had 12 little presents each in their Christmas stockings. How many presents did they have altogether?

yes or no?

5   92 infants came to the end-of-term concert. How many small chairs were needed in the school hall?

yes or no?

# More about multiplying.

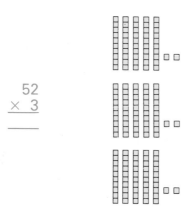

$$\begin{array}{r} 52 \\ \times\ 3 \\ \hline \end{array}$$

**Step 1.** Multiply to find how many units.

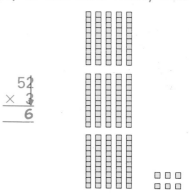

$$\begin{array}{r} 52 \\ \times\ 3 \\ \hline 6 \end{array}$$

**Step 2.** Multiply to find how many tens.

15 tens, or 1 hundred and 5 tens.

$$\begin{array}{r} 52 \\ \times\ 3 \\ \hline 156 \end{array}$$

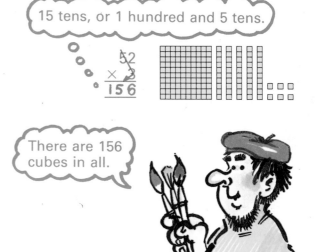

There are 156 cubes in all.

## Copy and complete.

| | | | | |
|---|---|---|---|---|
| 1 $\begin{array}{r} 42 \\ \times\ 3 \\ \hline \end{array}$ | 2 $\begin{array}{r} 21 \\ \times\ 5 \\ \hline \end{array}$ | 3 $\begin{array}{r} 52 \\ \times\ 4 \\ \hline \end{array}$ | 4 $\begin{array}{r} 43 \\ \times\ 3 \\ \hline \end{array}$ | 5 $\begin{array}{r} 64 \\ \times\ 2 \\ \hline \end{array}$ |
| 6 $\begin{array}{r} 41 \\ \times\ 4 \\ \hline \end{array}$ | 7 $\begin{array}{r} 50 \\ \times\ 3 \\ \hline \end{array}$ | 8 $\begin{array}{r} 54 \\ \times\ 2 \\ \hline \end{array}$ | 9 $\begin{array}{r} 62 \\ \times\ 4 \\ \hline \end{array}$ | 10 $\begin{array}{r} 31 \\ \times\ 5 \\ \hline \end{array}$ |
| 11 $\begin{array}{r} 31 \\ \times\ 7 \\ \hline \end{array}$ | 12 $\begin{array}{r} 73 \\ \times\ 3 \\ \hline \end{array}$ | 13 $\begin{array}{r} 21 \\ \times\ 6 \\ \hline \end{array}$ | 14 $\begin{array}{r} 50 \\ \times\ 8 \\ \hline \end{array}$ | 15 $\begin{array}{r} 40 \\ \times\ 6 \\ \hline \end{array}$ |

| 16 | 53<br>× 2 | 17 | 83<br>× 3 | 18 | 60<br>× 5 | 19 | 73<br>× 2 | 20 | 93<br>× 3 |
|----|-----------|----|-----------|----|-----------|----|-----------|----|-----------|
| 21 | 60<br>× 6 | 22 | 50<br>× 5 | 23 | 40<br>× 8 | 24 | 80<br>× 7 | 25 | 70<br>× 4 |

Give each product.

26  92 × 4          27  40 × 7          28  63 × 3

29  72 × 2          30  31 × 8          31  50 × 2

Copy and complete the table.

32

| Bottles | Refund |
|---------|--------|
| 22 | 88p |
| 12 | |
| 31 | |
| 42 | |
| 50 | |
| 61 | |

REFUND
4p per bottle

Solve.

33  A stamp costs 42p.
How much will 3 stamps cost?

34  A parcel weighs 21 kg.
What is the weight of 9 parcels?

35  A piece of ribbon is 52 cm long.
What is the total length of
4 pieces?

36  A bus fare is 61p.
How much would it
cost for 2 people?

37  A television programme lasts
30 minutes.
How long would 8 programmes
last?

38  There are 43 balloons in a packet.
How many balloons are there in
3 packets?

# Multiplication with regrouping.

Multiply 24 by 3.

$$\begin{array}{r} 24 \\ \times\ 3 \\ \hline \end{array}$$

**Step 1.**
Multiply 4 by 3.

**Step 2.**
Regroup the 12 units
as 1 ten and 2 units.

$$\begin{array}{r} 24 \\ \times\ 3 \\ \hline 2 \\ 1 \end{array}$$

**Step 3.**
Multiply 2 tens by 3.
2 tens multiplied by 3 = 6 tens.

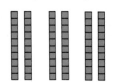

**Step 4.**
Add 6 tens and the 1 ten
from regrouping.
There are 7 tens.
The product is 72.

$$\begin{array}{r} 24 \\ \times\ 3 \\ \hline 72 \\ 1 \end{array}$$

Rounding may be used to help estimate a product.
An estimate can help you decide whether you have made a mistake.

$$\begin{array}{r} 29 \\ \times\ 3 \\ \hline \end{array}$$ Round to $$\begin{array}{r} 30 \\ \times\ 3 \\ \hline 90 \end{array}$$ $$\begin{array}{r} 29 \\ \times\ 3 \\ \hline 87 \\ 2 \end{array}$$ The estimate (90) and
the product (87) are
close to each other.

## Estimate first, then multiply.
Check your work again if the estimate and product are not close to each other.

1. $$\begin{array}{r} 36 \\ \times\ 2 \\ \hline \end{array}$$
2. $$\begin{array}{r} 18 \\ \times\ 4 \\ \hline \end{array}$$
3. $$\begin{array}{r} 17 \\ \times\ 5 \\ \hline \end{array}$$
4. $$\begin{array}{r} 12 \\ \times\ 7 \\ \hline \end{array}$$
5. $$\begin{array}{r} 14 \\ \times\ 5 \\ \hline \end{array}$$

6. $$\begin{array}{r} 16 \\ \times\ 6 \\ \hline \end{array}$$
7. $$\begin{array}{r} 49 \\ \times\ 2 \\ \hline \end{array}$$
8. $$\begin{array}{r} 13 \\ \times\ 7 \\ \hline \end{array}$$
9. $$\begin{array}{r} 25 \\ \times\ 3 \\ \hline \end{array}$$
10. $$\begin{array}{r} 29 \\ \times\ 4 \\ \hline \end{array}$$

11. $$\begin{array}{r} 37 \\ \times\ 2 \\ \hline \end{array}$$
12. $$\begin{array}{r} 19 \\ \times\ 4 \\ \hline \end{array}$$
13. $$\begin{array}{r} 26 \\ \times\ 3 \\ \hline \end{array}$$
14. $$\begin{array}{r} 45 \\ \times\ 2 \\ \hline \end{array}$$
15. $$\begin{array}{r} 28 \\ \times\ 3 \\ \hline \end{array}$$

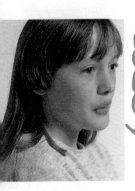

Here is another way of multiplying. It will help you to avoid making mistakes.

```
   48
 ×  7
   56   (8 × 7 = 56)
 +280   (40 × 7 = 280)
  336
```

But it is a longer way than on the last page.

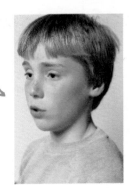

Multiply in the way you prefer.

16   78    × 3

17   65    × 7

18   73    × 6

19   48    × 3

20   68    × 7

21   56    × 5

22   84    × 8

23   93    × 6

24   39    × 3

25   47    × 9

26   63p    × 8

27   56p    × 2

28   62p    × 4

29   54p    × 9

30   83p    × 5

Solve.

31   4 days. How many hours?

32   8 hours. How many minutes?

33   24 weeks. How many days?

34   7 minutes. How many seconds?

35   A comic costs 18p. How much do 8 comics cost?

36   A book costs 85p. How much do 4 books cost?

37   An orange costs 5p. How much do 36 oranges cost?

38   An apple costs 7p. How much do 19 apples cost?

Here's how to multiply 54 × 3 in your head. Add 4 × 3 to 50 × 3. That's 12 plus 150 which is 162.

Multiply these in your head.

63 = 60 + 3

39   63 × 5

40   48 × 4

41   72 × 6

42   87 × 3

# Number problems.

Remember these steps to help
you solve number problems:

A  Read the problem and find
   the question.
B  What are the facts?
C  Decide what to do.
D  Answer the question.
E  Does your answer seem
   right?

Sue and Steve are helping
in a greengrocer's shop.

1  They had 200 tomatoes
   and sold 59.
   How many tomatoes
   were there left?

2  They had 420 apples.
   One day they sold 139 eating
   apples and 88 cooking apples.

   (a)  How many apples
        were sold altogether?

   (b)  How many apples remained?

3  Three customers each bought
   12 oranges. Steve took them
   out of a basket that contained
   170 oranges.
   How many were left in the basket?

4  One week Sue and Steve sold
   75 tomatoes a day. How many
   tomatoes did they sell in 6 days?

5  (a)  Mrs Ross bought 3 kilograms
        of peas for 65p a kilogram.
        What was the total cost?

   (b)  Mrs Ross paid with
        a £5.00 note. How much
        change did she get?

6 Mr Smith bought 4 pineapples costing £0.95 each. What was the total cost?

7 (a) Miss Peck bought 6 cauliflowers costing 46p each and 3 melons costing 67p each. What was the total cost?

(b) She paid with a £5.00 note. How much change did she get?

8 What is the total cost of:
(a) 5 cucumbers costing 42p each?
(b) 7 oranges costing 16p each?
(c) 4 bananas costing 14p each?

9 Make up some prices of your own or find the cost of cauliflowers, grapefruit, cucumbers, oranges and bananas from a local supermarket. Make up some problems like 7 and 8 and give them to a friend to solve. Your friend can make up some problems for you.

## keeping skills sharp

| 1 | 2 | 3 | 4 | 5 |
|---|---|---|---|---|
| 68<br>−24 | 83<br>−36 | 90<br>−47 | 494<br>−216 | 501<br>−375 |

| 6 | 7 | 8 | 9 | 10 |
|---|---|---|---|---|
| 500<br>−178 | 7268<br>− 179 | 3895<br>−1978 | 8114<br>−2609 | 8004<br>−2769 |

## Multiplication of money.

Multiply £0.78 by 6.

**Method 1**   £0.78 = 78p

**Step 1.**
$$\begin{array}{r} 78p \\ \times\ 6 \\ \hline 8p \\ \hline ^4 \end{array}$$
(8 × 6 = 48)

**Step 2.**
$$\begin{array}{r} 78p \\ \times\ 6 \\ \hline 468p \\ \hline ^4 \end{array}$$
( 7 × 6 = 42)
(42 + 4 = 46)

This is the number of tens.

**Method 2**

**Step 1.**
$$\begin{array}{r} £0.78 \\ \times\ 6 \\ \hline 8 \\ \hline ^4 \end{array}$$
(8 × 6 = 48)

**Step 2.**
$$\begin{array}{r} £0.78 \\ \times\ 6 \\ \hline £4.68 \\ \hline ^4 \end{array}$$
( 7 × 6 = 42)
(42 + 4 = 46)

Multiply. Give your answers (a) in pence, (b) in pounds.

1
$$\begin{array}{r} 69p \\ \times\ 2 \\ \hline \end{array}$$

2
$$\begin{array}{r} 84p \\ \times\ 7 \\ \hline \end{array}$$

3
$$\begin{array}{r} 96p \\ \times\ 5 \\ \hline \end{array}$$

4
$$\begin{array}{r} 41p \\ \times\ 9 \\ \hline \end{array}$$

5
$$\begin{array}{r} 27p \\ \times\ 8 \\ \hline \end{array}$$

6
$$\begin{array}{r} 63p \\ \times\ 6 \\ \hline \end{array}$$

7
$$\begin{array}{r} 91p \\ \times\ 4 \\ \hline \end{array}$$

8
$$\begin{array}{r} 47p \\ \times\ 3 \\ \hline \end{array}$$

9
$$\begin{array}{r} 18p \\ \times\ 6 \\ \hline \end{array}$$

10
$$\begin{array}{r} 37p \\ \times\ 7 \\ \hline \end{array}$$

Multiply. Give your answers in pounds.

11
$$\begin{array}{r} £28 \\ \times\ 5 \\ \hline \end{array}$$

12
$$\begin{array}{r} £74 \\ \times\ 3 \\ \hline \end{array}$$

13
$$\begin{array}{r} £19 \\ \times\ 6 \\ \hline \end{array}$$

14
$$\begin{array}{r} £83 \\ \times\ 7 \\ \hline \end{array}$$

15
$$\begin{array}{r} £37 \\ \times\ 2 \\ \hline \end{array}$$

16
$$\begin{array}{r} £45 \\ \times\ 9 \\ \hline \end{array}$$

17
$$\begin{array}{r} £92 \\ \times\ 7 \\ \hline \end{array}$$

18
$$\begin{array}{r} £58 \\ \times\ 4 \\ \hline \end{array}$$

19
$$\begin{array}{r} £63 \\ \times\ 8 \\ \hline \end{array}$$

20
$$\begin{array}{r} £29 \\ \times\ 10 \\ \hline \end{array}$$

21
$$\begin{array}{r} £0.15 \\ \times\ 10 \\ \hline \end{array}$$

22
$$\begin{array}{r} £0.83 \\ \times\ 7 \\ \hline \end{array}$$

23
$$\begin{array}{r} £0.96 \\ \times\ 2 \\ \hline \end{array}$$

24
$$\begin{array}{r} £0.93 \\ \times\ 4 \\ \hline \end{array}$$

25
$$\begin{array}{r} £0.29 \\ \times\ 7 \\ \hline \end{array}$$

26 Multiply £28 by 9.    27 Multiply £0.47 by 6.    28 Multiply 9p by 82.

29 Multiply 8p by 40.    30 Multiply £7 by 46.    31 Multiply £6 by 95.

32 Find the cost:

(a) £14    Anita bought 8 jumpers.

(b) £0.62    Julie bought 7 paint brushes.

(c) 85p    Stuart bought 9 balls.

(d) 29p    Justin bought 10 bags.

(e) 8p    Clare bought 76 pencils.

33 A farmer bought 16 hens costing £7 each and 9 turkeys costing £14 each. What was the total cost?

34 Heather bought 8 oranges costing 14p each and 6 bananas costing 13p each. What was the total cost?

35 Find the total cost of buying 3 tins of beans at 28p a tin, 5 loaves at 36p each and 6 packets of soap powder at £0.74 each.

36 Find the price of some groceries at a local shop. Make up some bills like the one in question 35. Give them to a friend who has to find the total cost. You find the total cost of your friend's bills.

## ready or not?

| | | | | |
|---|---|---|---|---|
| 1  8)32 | 2  6)30 | 3  4)32 | 4  4)36 | 5  6)36 |
| 6  8)40 | 7  9)36 | 8  9)45 | 9  5)40 | 10  7)42 |
| 11  45 ÷ 5 | 12  56 ÷ 8 | 13  42 ÷ 6 | 14  56 ÷ 7 | 15  72 ÷ 9 |
| 16  48 ÷ 8 | 17  63 ÷ 7 | 18  48 ÷ 6 | 19  81 ÷ 9 | 20  54 ÷ 9 |

## Dividing a 2-digit number.

The examples show how to divide a 2-digit number.

### Example 1

Think about dividing up the blocks.

3)69

**Step 1.** Divide the tens.

$$\begin{array}{r} 2 \\ 3{\overline{\smash{\big)}\,69}} \end{array}$$

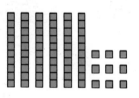

**Step 2.** Divide the units.

Number in each set

$$\begin{array}{r} 23 \\ 3{\overline{\smash{\big)}\,69}} \end{array}$$

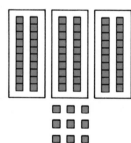

Number of sets

### Example 2

2)80

**Step 1.** Divide the tens.

$$\begin{array}{r} 4 \\ 2{\overline{\smash{\big)}\,80}} \end{array}$$

**Step 2.** Divide the units.

$$\begin{array}{r} 40 \\ 2{\overline{\smash{\big)}\,80}} \end{array}$$

The answer, 40, is called the **quotient**.
Why is it important to write the zero?

Divide.

1. $2\overline{)42}$     2. $4\overline{)40}$     3. $2\overline{)68}$     4. $5\overline{)55}$     5. $2\overline{)62}$

6. $6\overline{)66}$     7. $3\overline{)33}$     8. $4\overline{)88}$     9. $2\overline{)86}$     10. $4\overline{)44}$

11. $2\overline{)80}$     12. $3\overline{)63}$     13. $2\overline{)44}$     14. $3\overline{)36}$     15. $2\overline{)88}$

16. $84 \div 4$     17. $48 \div 4$     18. $66 \div 3$     19. $84 \div 2$     20. $46 \div 2$

21. $30 \div 3$     22. $64 \div 2$     23. $39 \div 3$     24. $80 \div 4$     25. $99 \div 3$

26. This is a page from Beth's book.
Which did she get wrong?
What mistake did she make?

1. $2\overline{)86}$ gives $43$     2. $4\overline{)40}$ gives $1$

3. $3\overline{)96}$ gives $32$     4. $2\overline{)62}$ gives $31$

27.

How many pencils can you buy?

28.

How many rubbers can you buy?

29. Bill divided up 48 marbles.
He put the same number of
marbles in each of 2 boxes.
How many marbles did he put
in each box?

30. Sonia found 66 seashells.
She shared them equally with
her 2 sisters. How many seashells
did each child get?

31. Division can be checked by multiplication.
For example, $28 \div 2 = 14$. Check: $14 \times 2 = 28$.
Check your answers to questions 1 to 25 by multiplication.

# Division with regrouping.

Sometimes you will need to regroup when dividing.
In the example, 2 tens are regrouped as 20 units.

3)81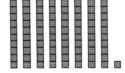

**Step 1.** Divide the tens.
There are are 2 tens
in each of the 3 sets.
6 tens are used up.

2 tens and
1 unit left.

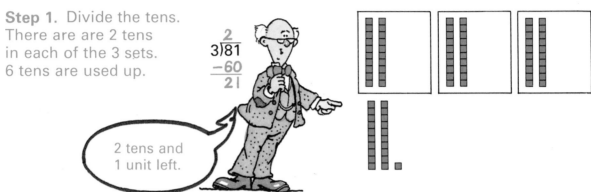

**Step 2.** Regroup
2 tens as 20 units.

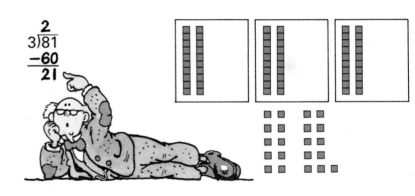

**Step 3.** Divide the units.

There are 7 units
in each of the 3 sets.
21 units are used up.

Copy and complete.

| 1 | 2 | 3 | 4 | 5 |
|---|---|---|---|---|
| 15 | 26 | 1 | 1 | |
| 3)45 | 2)52 | 4)72 | 5)75 | 6)72 |
| −30 | −40 | −40 | −50 | − |
| 15 | 12 | | | |
| − | − | − | − | − |

Divide.

6  6)84          7  2)64          8  3)57          9  3)84          10  6)90

11  4)68         12  2)74         13  5)70         14  3)87         15  8)96

16  7)91         17  5)60         18  4)88         19  3)54         20  5)95

21  80 ÷ 4       22  42 ÷ 3       23  96 ÷ 6       24  85 ÷ 5       25  78 ÷ 3

26  96 ÷ 2       27  90 ÷ 5       28  98 ÷ 7       29  80 ÷ 5       30  78 ÷ 6

Solve.

31  84 days.
How many weeks?

32  65 toes.
How many feet?

33  58 ears.
How many people?

34  48 sides.
How many triangles?

Find the end number.

35  START

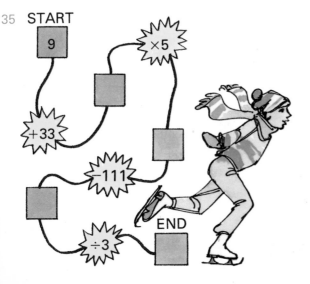

36  START

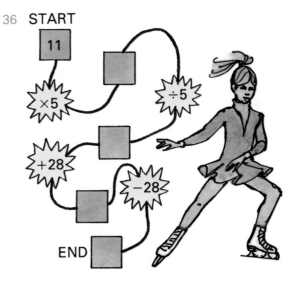

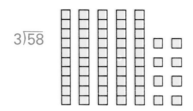

**Step 1.** Divide the tens. Subtract.

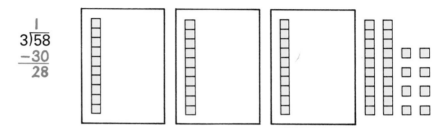

**Step 2.** Regroup.

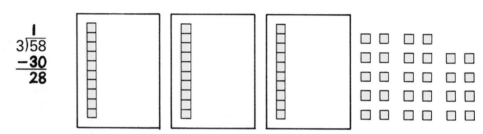

**Step 3.** Divide the units. Subtract.

This number is called the **remainder.**

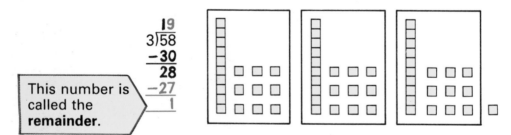

**Step 4.** Write the remainder.

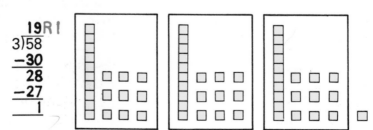

First estimate the quotient, then divide.
See if your answer makes sense.

1  $3\overline{)49}$  2  $5\overline{)58}$  3  $4\overline{)63}$  4  $3\overline{)38}$  5  $6\overline{)77}$

6  $4\overline{)72}$  7  $5\overline{)74}$  8  $7\overline{)79}$  9  $8\overline{)86}$  10  $5\overline{)68}$

11  $6\overline{)60}$  12  $3\overline{)78}$  13  $6\overline{)84}$  14  $3\overline{)71}$  15  $4\overline{)81}$

16  $4\overline{)69}$  17  $7\overline{)89}$  18  $5\overline{)72}$  19  $8\overline{)99}$  20  $6\overline{)75}$

21  $92 \div 3$  22  $73 \div 5$  23  $53 \div 4$  24  $95 \div 3$  25  $97 \div 7$

26  $97 \div 5$  27  $91 \div 6$  28  $68 \div 3$  29  $98 \div 4$  30  $92 \div 4$

31  How much for each child if
the money is shared equally?

32  How much for each child if
the money is shared equally?

33  82 bottles altogether.
6 bottles in a pack.
How many packs are needed?
How many bottles are left over?

34  95 bottles altogether.
8 bottles in a pack.
How many packs are needed?
How many bottles are left over?

35  58 wheels.
4 wheels for each car.
How many cars?
How many wheels left over?

36  85 days.
7 days in a week.
How many weeks?
How many days left over?

# Division of money.

A   Three children have £0.79 to share.
How much should they have if
they all receive the same amount?
How much will be left?

```
      26
  3)79
    −60
     19
    −18
      1
```
They get 26p each and there
is 1p left.

B   A balloon costs 5p. How many balloons
can Ben buy with 62p?
How much money would he have left?

```
      12
  5)62
    −50
     12
    −10
      2
```
Ben could buy 12 balloons.
He would have 2p left.

Divide.

1  2)64p       2  3)96p       3  5)50p       4  4)84p       5  3)60p

6  3)£60       7  2)£46       8  2)£81.00     9  5)£53.00     10  4)£49.00

11  Two girls share £4.60 equally.
How much will they each get?

12  Two boys share £2.40 equally.
How much will each boy get?

13  How many books, costing £5 each,
can Mr. Blunt buy with £48?
How much would he have left?

14  How many plants, costing
£3 each, can Mrs. Smith buy
with £23?
How much would she have left?

15  How many pencils, costing 10p,
can Emma buy with 95p?
How much would she have left?

# Multiplication and division puzzle.

| A | B | C | D | E | F | G | H | I | J | K | L | M |
|---|---|---|---|---|---|---|---|---|---|---|---|---|
| 4 | 21 | 7 | 48 | 24 | 81 | 3 | 10 | 35 | 8 | 61 | 42 | 5 |

| N | O | P | Q | R | S | T | U | V | W | X | Y | Z |
|---|---|---|---|---|---|---|---|---|---|---|---|---|
| 9 | 28 | 1 | 19 | 36 | 12 | 6 | 23 | 41 | 15 | 87 | 43 | 29 |

Multiply or divide.
Copy and complete. The answers to the questions will then appear.

1   What has six legs, two heads and a tail?

| $2 \times 2$ | $4\overline{)20}$ | $12 \div 3$ | $3 \times 3$ | $4 \times 7$ | $3\overline{)27}$ | $20 \div 5$ |
|---|---|---|---|---|---|---|
| 4 | | | | | | |
| A | | | | | | |

| $30 \div 3$ | $7 \times 4$ | $6 \times 6$ | $3 \times 4$ | $4 \times 6$ |
|---|---|---|---|---|
| | | | | |
| | | | | |

2   What goes 99 clonk, 99 clonk, 99 clonk?

| $4\overline{)16}$ | $5\overline{)35}$ | $3 \times 8$ | $6\overline{)54}$ | $60 \div 10$ | $7 \times 5$ | $8 \div 8$ | $4 \times 6$ | $6 \times 8$ | $8 \times 3$ |
|---|---|---|---|---|---|---|---|---|---|
| | | | | | | | | | |
| | | | | | | | | | |

| $3 \times 5$ | $5 \times 7$ | $12 \div 2$ | $5\overline{)50}$ | $4 \div 1$ |
|---|---|---|---|---|
| | | | | |
| | | | | |

| $5 \times 3$ | $4 \times 7$ | $7 \times 4$ | $8 \times 6$ | $6 \times 4$ | $45 \div 5$ | $7 \times 6$ | $3 \times 8$ | $24 \div 8$ |
|---|---|---|---|---|---|---|---|---|
| | | | | | | | | |
| | | | | | | | | |

1   Measure each length to the nearest centimetre:

(a)

(b)

2   Draw lines of these lengths:

(a)   **10 cm**        (b)   **4 cm**         (c)   between **7 cm** and **8 cm**

(d)   between **6 cm** and **7 cm** but nearer to **6 cm** than to **7 cm**

3   Copy and complete:

(a)   **600 cm** = .... **m**          (b)   **145 cm** = .... **m** .... **cm**

(c)   **4 m** = .... **cm**            (d)   **3 m 9 cm** = .... **cm**

4   Copy and complete:

(a)   **2 km** = .... **m**            (b)   **4000 m** = .... **km**

(c)   **1 km 620 m** = .... **m**       (d)   **9760 m** = .... **km** .... **m**

5   Measure these to the nearest centimetre:

(a)   **your arm span**          (b)   **your height**

(c)   **your hand span**         (d)   **your normal pace**

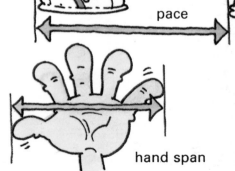

pace

arm span

hand span

6   How long do you think it would take you to walk 1 km?
    Choose from the four answers below.

A   60 minutes       B   14 minutes       C   3 minutes       D   35 minutes

1  Measure the sides and find the perimeters of these shapes:

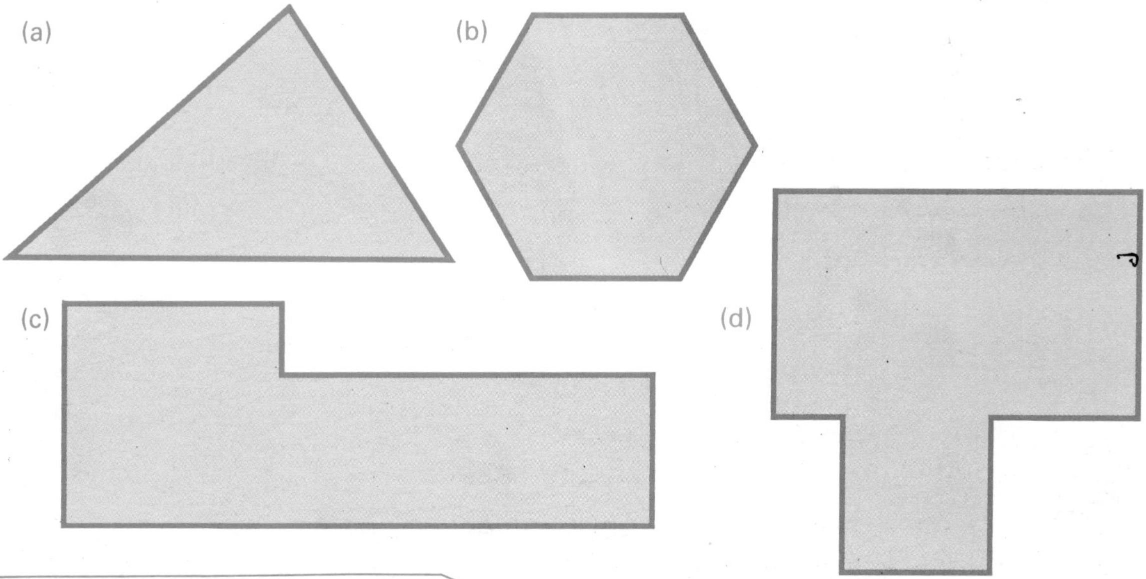

(a)

(b)

(c)

(d)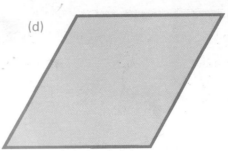

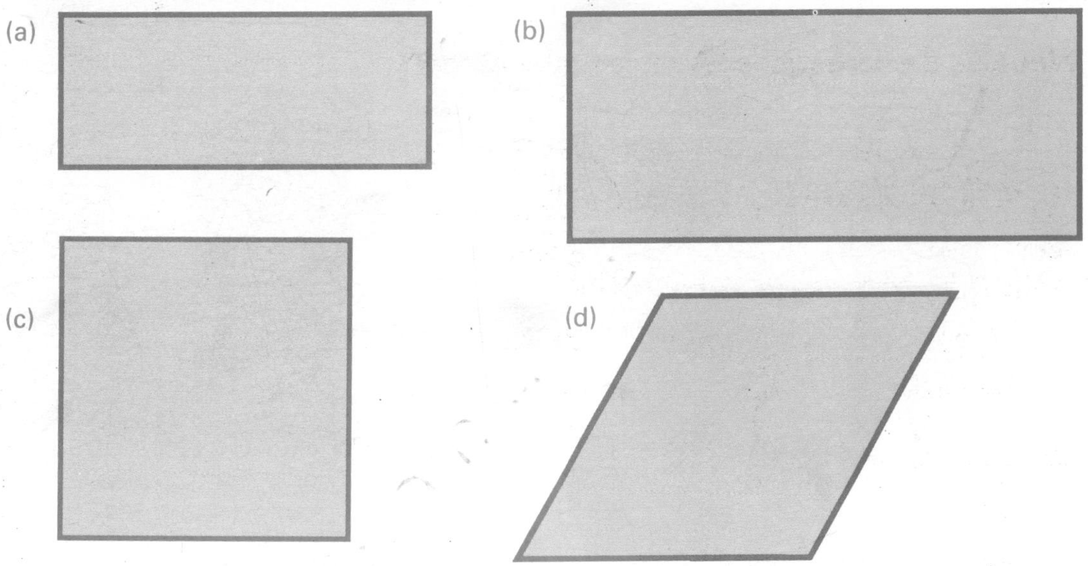

2  Find the perimeters of these shapes:

(a)

(b)

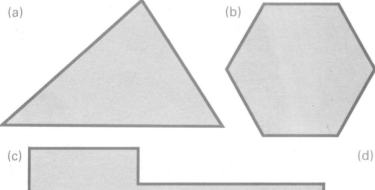

(c)

(d)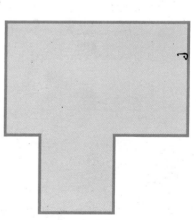

1   Who has the larger shoe?

(a)   How many circles does
Ashraf's shoe cover?

(b)   How many circles does
Wendy's shoe cover?

(c)   Who has the larger shoe?

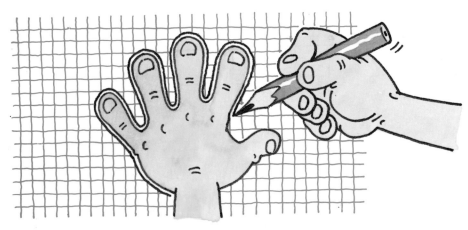

2   You will need some squared paper.
Draw round your hand on the squared paper.

(a)   How many squares does your hand cover?

(b)   Find the size of some friends' hands.
Make a chart like this:

| Name | Number of squares |
|---|---|
| My hand | 73 |
| Jon's hand | 81 |
| Alice's hand | 72 |
| | |

This is one unit square.

The area is one square unit.

Find the areas.

1

Area = _6_ square units.

2

Area = ___ square units.

3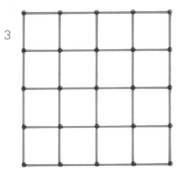

Area = ___ square units.

4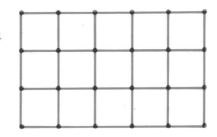

Area = ___ square units.

5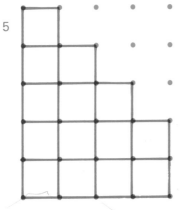

Area = ___ square units.

6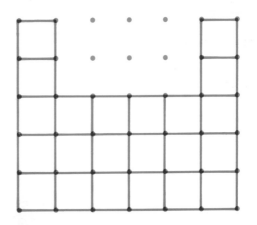

Area = ___ square units.

To find the area of this rectangle
we will use
this square
as a unit.

1 cm 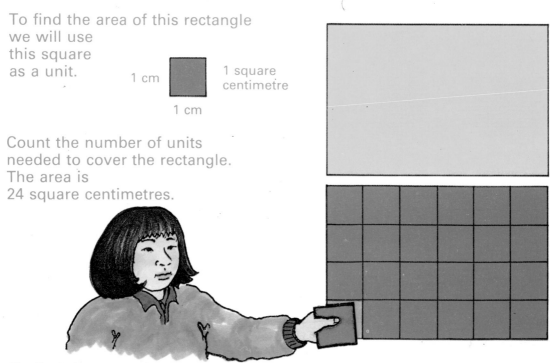 1 square
centimetre
1 cm

Count the number of units
needed to cover the rectangle.
The area is
24 square centimetres.

To find the area of rectangles you can multiply.

There are 6 columns of 4 squares each.

There are 6 × 4 = 24 squares.

    Area = length × breadth

    Area = 6 cm × 4 cm = 24 square centimetres.

Square centimetres can be written as cm² so the area is 24 cm².

**Give each area:**

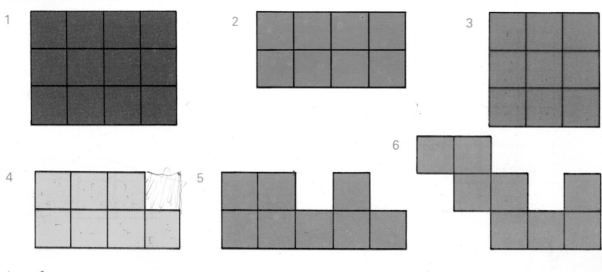

1      2      3

4      5      6

7  Copy the table.
   Find the area of
   the rectangles.
   Complete the table.

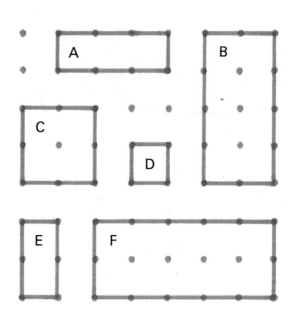

| | A | B | C | D | E | F |
|---|---|---|---|---|---|---|
| Length in cm | 3 | | | | | |
| Breadth in cm | 1 | | | | | |
| Area in square cm | 3 | | | | | |

8  You need some
   centimetre-squared paper.
   Draw these rectangles.
   Then find their area.

   (a)  8 cm long, 3 cm wide.      (b)  10 cm long, 2 cm wide.

   (c)  5 cm long, 4 cm wide.      (d)  12 cm long, 1 cm wide.

   (e)  6 cm long, 5 cm wide.      (f)  9 cm long, 7 cm wide.

9  Use centimetre-squared
   paper. Draw some shapes that
   have an area of 12 cm$^2$.

10  A rectangular garden plot is
    9 m long and 7 m wide.
    What is the area?

11  One side of a square is 8 m.
    What is its area?

12  A room has an area of
    72 square metres. Its length is
    9 metres. What is its breadth?

Give each area.

13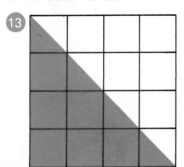

14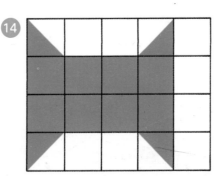

15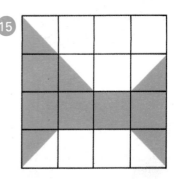

### Rectangles and prime numbers.

A rectangle has 4 sides.
All of its angles are right angles.
Its opposite sides are equal.

A square has 4 equal
sides and all of its
angles are right angles.
A square is a special
kind of rectangle.

Look at the illustration on the right.
For each number the same number
of small squares has been drawn.

If the number of small squares
can only be made into one
rectangle then that number
is a **prime number**.

If the number of small squares
can be made into more than one
rectangle, then the number
is **not** a prime number.

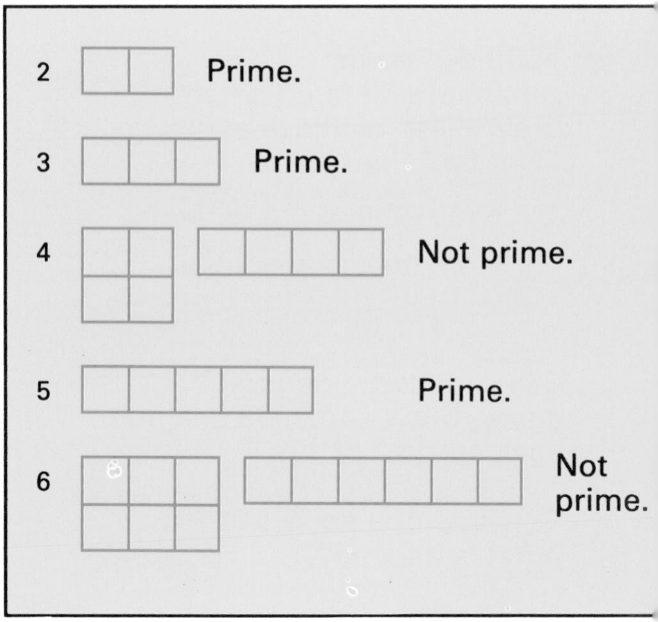

1 is a special case and is
**not** a prime number.

2   Prime.

3   Prime.

4   Not prime.

5   Prime.

6   Not prime.

1   You need some centimetre-squared paper.
Copy these shapes on to squared paper.

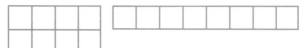

   (a)   Is 7 a prime number?      (b)   Is 8 a prime number?

2   Draw rectangles or squares for 9 and 10.
Write whether they are prime numbers or not.

Some of the rectangles for the following numbers have been drawn.

Draw any rectangles that are missing. Each missing rectangle is shown by

The total number of rectangles is given.
(Rectangles include squares.)

| Number | How many rectangles? | | Prime or not prime? |
|--------|---------------------|---|---------------------|
| 11 | 1 | 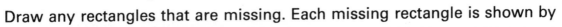 | Prime |
| 12 | 3 | | |
| 13 | 1 | | |
| 14 | 2 | | |
| 15 | 2 | | |
| 16 | 3 | | |
| 17 | 1 | | |
| 18 | 3 | | |
| 19 | 1 | | |
| 20 | 3 | | |
| 21 | 2 | | |

Continue until you reach 30.

## Volume.

Find the volume of this box.
Use this
cube as
a unit.

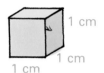

1 cm
1 cm
1 cm

Count the number of units
needed to fill the box.
One unit cube is called
a cubic centimetre.
This is written as cm³.
The volume of
the box is 16 cm³.

To find the volume of a box like the one shown above
you can count the number of units.
A quicker way is to multiply.
There are 4 × 2 blocks in a layer.
There are 2 layers.

Volume = 4 × 2 × 2 = 16 cubic blocks

Volume = 4 cm × 2 cm × 2 cm = 16 cm³.

## Find each volume.

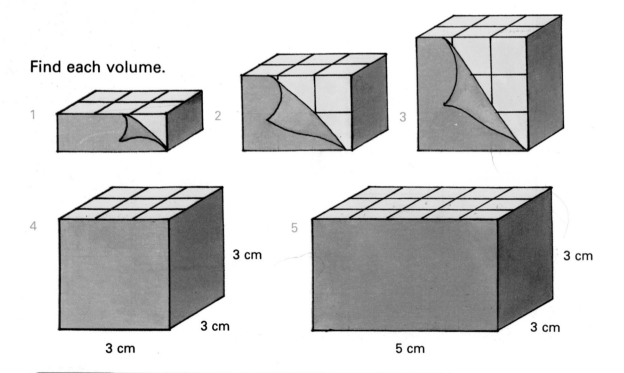

1

2

3

4
3 cm
3 cm
3 cm

5
3 cm
3 cm
5 cm

6    4 cm    2 cm    3 cm

7    5 cm    2 cm    3 cm

8    6 cm    2 cm    2 cm

9    4 cm    2 cm    5 cm

Are these questions about **length, area,** or **volume**?

10   How much string do you have?

11   How much sand will the bucket hold?

12   How much paper is needed to cover the display board?

## Volume, capacity and weight.

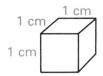

A cube with edges of 1 cm has a volume of 1 cubic centimetre.
(1 cm³ = 1 cubic centimetre)

If this cube had no top and we filled it with water it would hold
1 millilitre of water. (We write millilitre as ml.)

1 cm³ = 1 ml.
1 ml of water weighs 1 gram (1 g).

1 litre = 1000 millilitres.
1 l = 1000 ml.

Also 1 kilogram = 1000 grams (1 kg = 1000 g).

Here is a way of finding the weight of a litre of water.
You need a cube with sides 10 cm.

A   Fill your cube with dry sand.

B   Pour the sand into a jar or bottle.
Mark the level it comes up to.

C   Pour out the sand.

D   Pour the water into the bottle until
it comes up to the mark you made.
You then have 1 litre of water.

E   Weigh the water and bottle
together.

F   Pour out the water and weigh
the empty bottle.

G   Subtract to find the weight of 1 litre of water.
Weight = (weight of water and bottle) − (weight of bottle).
Your answer should be close to a kilogram.

## keeping skills sharp

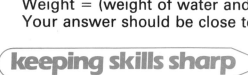

| 1 | 32<br>× 3 | 2 | 46<br>× 2 | 3 | 58<br>× 4 | 4 | 62<br>× 5 | 5 | 84<br>× 6 |

6  76 × 8      7  93 × 9      8  89 × 7

1   Write down the weight in grams of these amounts of water:

   (a)  20 cm³   (b)  49 cm³   (c)  51 cm³

   (d)  16 ml   (e)  60 ml

2   How many millilitres of water weigh:

   (a)  82 g   (b)  9 g   (c)  76 g

   (d)  $\frac{1}{2}$ kg   (e)  $\frac{1}{4}$ kg?

3   Find the volume of a stone.

   You need a metric measuring jug.

   Remember 1 ml = 1 cm³.

**Step A**

Put some water in the jug.
Write down the volume of water.

**Step B**

Put the stone in the jug.
Make sure there is enough water
to completely cover the stone.
If not start again.
Write down the volume shown by
the top of the water.
The water level will be higher.

**Step C**   Subtract the volume in **Step A** from the volume in **Step B**.
The answer is the volume of the stone.
Write down the volume.

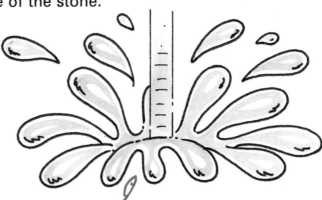

4   Find some stones or other objects
that will sink in water.
Calculate their volumes by
the method in question 3.

# Weight.

Some children weighed themselves on a kilogram scale.
They wrote their names and weights on slips of paper.

1  How many weigh 34 kg?

2  How many weigh
   more than 35 kg?

3  Who weighs the least?

4  Who weighs the same as Terry?

5  What is the total weight of
   John, Craig and Dave?

6  How many weigh
   more than Ann?

7  How many weigh
   less than Alan?

8  Find three children with a
   total weight of 100 kg.

Copy this table.

| Name | Weight to the nearest kilogram |
|------|--------------------------------|
| 1 | |
| 2 | |
| 3 | |
| 4 | |
| 5 | |
| 6 | |
| 7 | |
| 8 | |
| 9 | |
| Total weight | |

9 Find the weight of 9 people in your class. Round each person's weight to the nearest kilogram and enter their names and weights on your table.

10 Find the total weight of the 9 people.

11 Answer questions 1, 2, 3 and 7 for the people you weighed.

12 Write the table again with the people in order of weight; start with the heaviest.

13 How many children weigh

(a) 33 kg or less?
(b) 34 or 35 kg?
(c) 36 or 37 kg?
(d) 38 kg or more?

14 Draw a bar graph of the results of question 13.
Use 2 cm for each of the divisions (a), (b), (c) and (d).
Use 2 cm for each person.
Make up some questions based on your graph.
Give them to a friend to answer.
You answer your friend's questions.

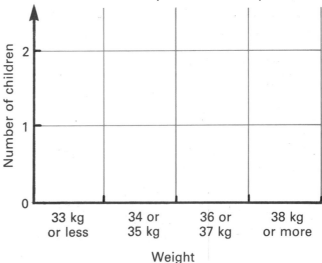

Ahmed and Julie made a tally chart to show the birthday months for the pupils in their year.

I I I I stands for 4.

⊦⊦⊦⊦ stands for 5.

18 would be recorded as ⊦⊦⊦⊦ ⊦⊦⊦⊦ ⊦⊦⊦⊦ I I I.

The total of the tallies is called the **frequency**.

**Example**

| Month | Tallies | Frequency |
|-------|---------|-----------|
| January | ⊦⊦⊦⊦ I I | 7 |

1   Copy and complete this tally chart.

| Month | Tallies | |
|-------|---------|---|
| January | ⊦⊦⊦⊦ I I | 7 |
| February | ⊦⊦⊦⊦ ⊦⊦⊦⊦ | |
| March | ⊦⊦⊦⊦ I I I I | |
| April | ⊦⊦⊦⊦ ⊦⊦⊦⊦ I I I | |
| May | ⊦⊦⊦⊦ ⊦⊦⊦⊦ ⊦⊦⊦⊦ | |
| June | | 11 |
| July | | 8 |
| August | | 10 |
| September | I I | |
| October | | 4 |
| November | | 5 |
| December | I I I | |

What is the total of the frequencies?

2   Make a tally chart for the children in your class showing the months they were born in.

Julie and Ahmed have drawn a block graph to show the results from question 1 on page 32.

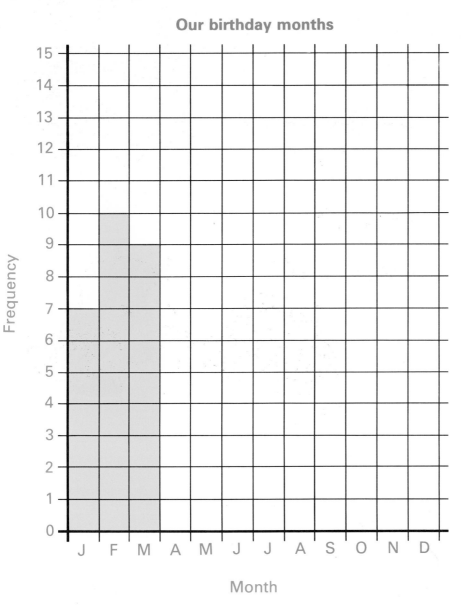

**Our birthday months**

3   Copy the block graph above on to centimetre-squared paper. Use the information from question 1 and complete the block graph.

4   Draw a block graph to show the information you collected for question 2.

5   Work with a friend. Make up questions based on the block graphs and answer them.

# Days and weeks.

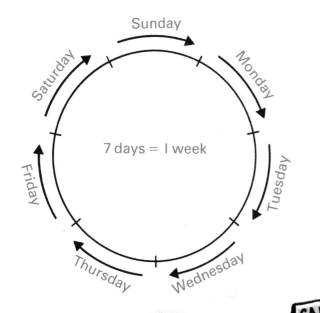

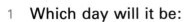
7 days = I week

**Example**
It is Monday.
What day will it be
in 10 days time?

Start at Monday.
Move 10 spaces in the
direction of the arrows.

You finish on Thursday.

10 days after Monday is
Thursday.

1 Which day will it be:

  (a) **8 days after Tuesday?**
  (b) **11 days after Friday?**
  (c) **14 days after Sunday?**

2 What day will it be:

  (a) **4 days before Sunday?**
  (b) **8 days before Wednesday?**
  (c) **10 days before Monday?**

(*Hint:* Move the opposite
way to the arrows.)

3 How many days in:

  (a) **2 weeks?**   (b) **4 weeks?**
  (c) **7 weeks?**   (d) **9 weeks?**
  (e) **10 weeks?**
  (f) **1 week 2 days?**
  (g) **2 weeks 1 day?**
  (h) **3 weeks 4 days?**
  (i) **4 weeks 6 days?**

4 Change to weeks and days:

**Example**
39 days    $39 \div 7 = 5$ R4
39 days = 5 weeks 4 days

  (a) **11 days**   (b) **16 days**
  (c) **27 days**   (d) **32 days**
  (e) **46 days**   (f) **53 days**

5 January has 31 days. $31 \div 7 = 4$ R3. January has 4 weeks 3 days.
Give the number of weeks and days in the other months.
(Count February as 28 days if it is not a leap year and 29 days if it is.)

| **January, 1991** | | | | | | |
|---|---|---|---|---|---|---|
| Su | M | Tu | W | Th | F | Sa |
|  |  | 1 | 2 | 3 | 4 | 5 |
| 6 | 7 | 8 | 9 | 10 | 11 | 12 |
| 13 | 14 | 15 | 16 | 17 | 18 | 19 |
| 20 | 21 | 22 | 23 | 24 | 25 | 26 |
| 27 | 28 | 29 | 30 | 31 |  |  |

| **February, 1991** | | | | | | |
|---|---|---|---|---|---|---|
| Su | M | Tu | W | Th | F | Sa |
|  |  |  |  |  | 1 | 2 |
| 3 | 4 | 5 | 6 | 7 | 8 | 9 |
| 10 | 11 | 12 | 13 | 14 | 15 | 16 |
| 17 | 18 | 19 | 20 | 21 | 22 | 23 |
| 24 | 25 | 26 | 27 | 28 |  |  |

How many days are there from January 14th to January 16th?

From the 14th to the 15th is one day.
From the 15th to the 16th is one day.

It is therefore 2 days from January 14th to January 16th.

We could have got the answer by subtracting (16 − 14 = 2).

---

*Important note*

If you count the 14th, 15th and 16th there are 3 days.
We only do this if we are **told** to include both the given dates.
Normally we include only **one** of the given dates.
(Calculations are made easier if you include the second date.)

---

**Example**

How many days are there from January 24th to February 3rd?
There are 7 days in January (31 − 24 = 7). There are 3 days in February.
Number of days from January 24th to February 3rd = 7 + 3 = 10.

1   How many days are there from:

(a)  February 1st to February 27th?     (b)  January 9th to January 31st?

(c)  January 26th to February 8th?     (d)  January 14th to February 20th?

2   Find the number of days from:

(a)  May 18th to June 6th.     (b)  July 2nd to August 14th.

(c)  November 5th to December 25th.   (d)  September 10th to October 25th.

3   How many days from December 25th to January 12th in the next year?

1  How many rectangles of any size
   can you find in this shape?

   Remember: a square is a rectangle.

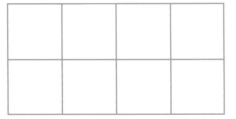

2

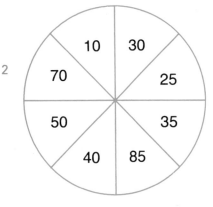

This is a special kind of dart board.
You throw four darts and each dart scores.
How many ways are there of scoring 130?
(The order does not matter so 50, 40, 30, 10
counts the same as 30, 10, 40, 50).

3  You start at the bottom left-hand corner
   and move vertically ↑ or horizontally →
   from one circle to one touching it.
   You finish at the top right-hand corner.
   You must 'collect' exactly nine numbers.
   (The first will be 6 and the last will be 6).
   What is the greatest total you can make?

FINISH

6 3 5 6 6 ◄
7 4 6 7 3
3 7 7 4 7
5 6 4 3 4
► 6 3 3 5 6

START

4  Use your calculator to help you answer these questions.
   (Consecutive numbers differ by 1. For example 58, 59, 60, 61.)

   (a)  What four consecutive numbers have a total of 98?

   (b)  756 is the result of multiplying two consecutive numbers.
        What are these numbers?

5  Scrooge used 216 candles.
   He saved all the ends and
   melted them down. 6 melted
   down ends made one candle.

   How many candles will Scrooge
   get out of his 216 ends?
   (*No*. The answer is not 36!)

1  Sarah cooked 56 cakes.
   She put 8 in each tray.
   How many trays did she need?

2  Sam made 78 sweets, Mary made 94 and James made 86.
   How many sweets did they make altogether?

3  9 children each made 7 fudge bars.
   How many bars were made altogether?

4  Jane had 1 kilogram of flour. She used 785 grams.
   (1 kilogram = 1000 grams.)
   How many grams were left?

5  A fruit cake costs £1.87.
   What is the cost of 3 cakes?

6  A birthday cake cost £3.64.
   What was the change from £10?

7  Denis had 42p.
   He bought as many biscuits costing 6p each as he could.
   How many biscuits did he buy?

8  Tessa had £1.00.
   She bought some gingerbread men costing 9p each.

   (a)  What is the greatest number she could buy?

   (b)  How much change would she get?

9  Half a litre of lemonade costs 36p.
   What is the cost of:

   (a)  1 litre?     (b)  2 litres?

10  A tray holds 6 jam tarts. John made 40 tarts.

   (a)  How many full trays did he use?

   (b)  How many trays did he need?

11  Paul bought 6 muffins at 10p each and 7 fruit buns
    at 9p each. How much did he spend?

12  Barbara spent 60p.
    28p was spent on crisps and the rest on chews.
    The chews cost 4p each.
    How many chews did she buy?

# More problems.

1   Sarah had 2 helpings of chips at 28p each.

   (a)   How much did she spend?

   (b)   How much change did she have out of £1?

2   Jo had 52p. She wanted to buy a milk shake for 24p and an ice-cream for 27p. Did she have enough money?

3   Roger had £3. He bought 2 sausage rolls costing 28p each and a drink costing 29p.

   (a)   How much did he spend?

   (b)   How much did he have left?

4   There were 32 children in a class.
$\frac{1}{4}$ went home for dinner, $\frac{1}{2}$ had
dinner at school,
the rest had sandwiches.
How many had:

   (a)   dinner at home?

   (b)   dinner at school?

   (c)   sandwiches?

5   There were 4 chairs at each table in a café.
How many chairs are needed for:

   (a)   3 tables?

   (b)   7 tables?

   (c)   10 tables?

6   A school shop had
900 cans of orange.
On Monday 146 were sold.
On Tuesday 239 were sold.

   (a)   How many were sold?

   (b)   How many remained?

7   Find the total cost of
7 cakes at 9p each,
3 drinks at 10p each
and 2 biscuits at 3p each.

**8** Bill, Mick and Elroy had a meal.
The total cost was £6.
Bill paid $\frac{1}{2}$.
Mick paid $\frac{1}{3}$.
Elroy paid the rest.
How much did:

(a) Elroy pay?  (b) Mick pay?  (c) Bill pay?

(d) What fraction of the £6 did Elroy pay?

**9** Chris bought some meat costing £1.60
and a pie costing 94p.
She had 48p left.

(a) How much did she spend?

(b) How much did she start with?

**10** A food hamper was sold at a sale.

(a) How much was
taken off the price?

(b) What is the sale price?

**11** A cake was cut into 16 equal pieces.
William ate 5 pieces.
Elizabeth ate 2 pieces.
Patrick ate $\frac{1}{4}$ of the cake.

(a) How many pieces did Patrick eat?

(b) How many pieces
were eaten altogether?

(c) What fraction of the cake was eaten?

(d) What fraction of the cake remained?

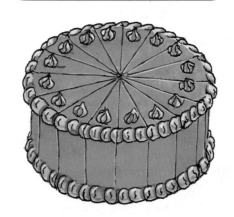

Measure these to
the nearest centimetre.

1    2    3    4    5

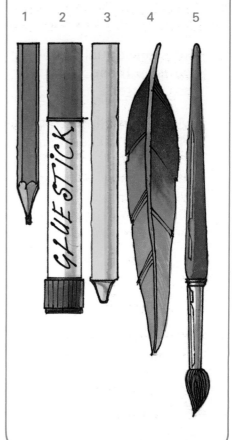

GLUE STICK

A  Draw a circle and cut it out.

B  Fold it in half.

C  Fold it in half again. It is now folded into four equal parts — these are quarters.

D  Open it out.

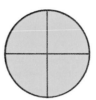

E  Make a small hole at the centre, O. Put a thin piece of string through it. Tie a knot in the string at the back of the circle.

F  Start with the string along the line OA.

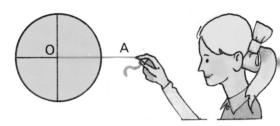

G  Move the string round the circle in the direction shown. Keep the string tight so that it is in a straight line.

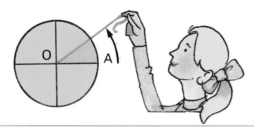

H  Continue to move the string round the circle until you have moved it through a right angle from OA.

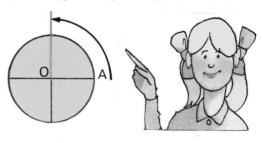

I  Fold the circle again to make a quarter.

J  Fold it in half again. The angle is half of a right angle.

K  Open out the circle.

half a right angle.

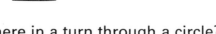

1  How many right angles are there in a turn through a circle?

2  How many half right angles are there in a turn through a circle?

# Naming angles.

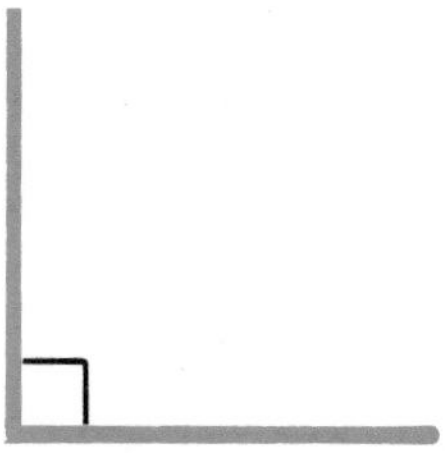

A **right angle**.

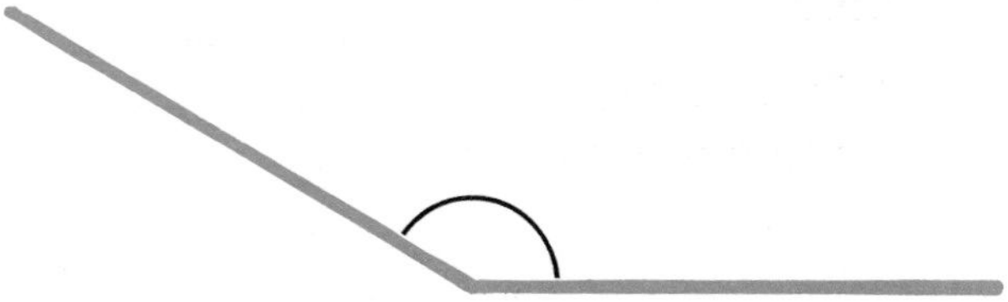

An **obtuse angle** is greater than a right angle, but less than two right angles.

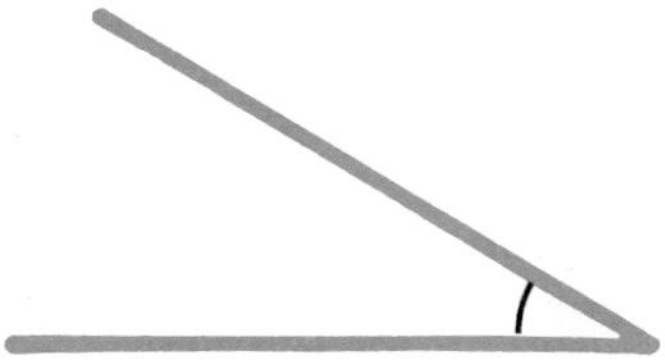

An **acute angle** is less than a right angle.

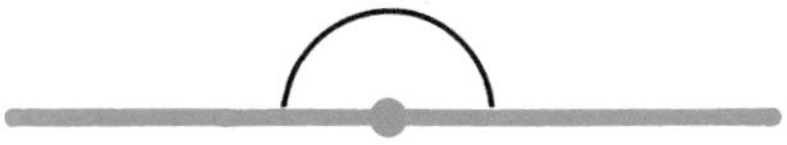

A **straight−line angle** (or **straight angle**) equals two right angles.

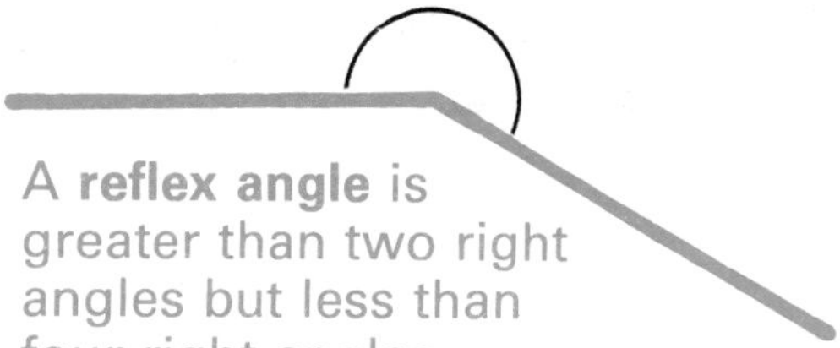

A **reflex angle** is greater than two right angles but less than four right angles.

Fold a piece of paper to form a right angle.
Use your right angle to find which of these angles are:

(a) right angles;　　(b) acute angles;　　(c) obtuse angles;　　(d) reflex angles.

1

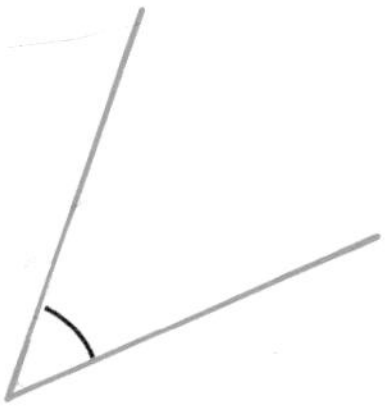

2

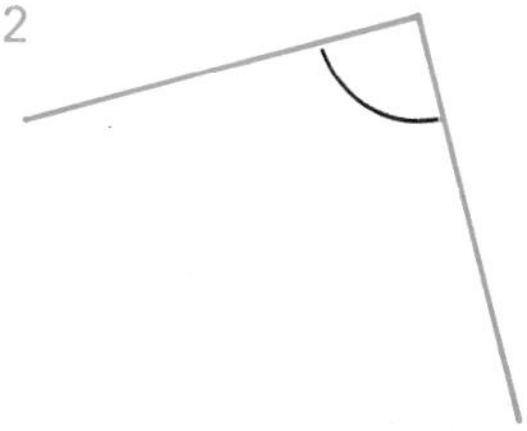

3

4

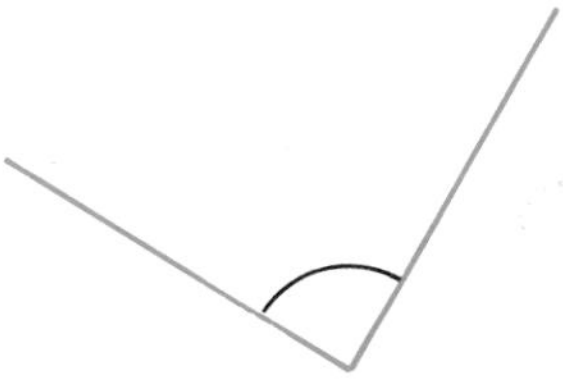

5

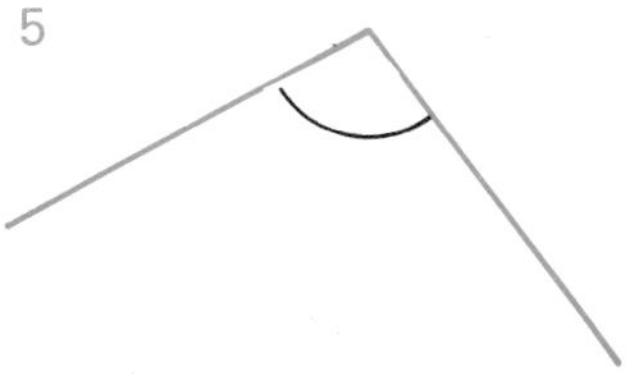

6

7

8

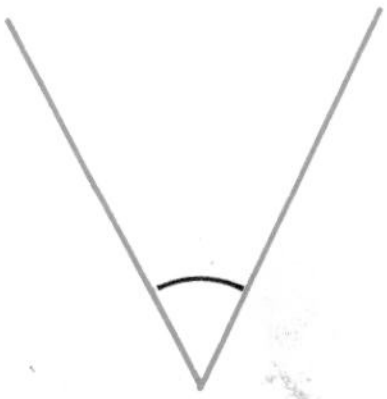

9

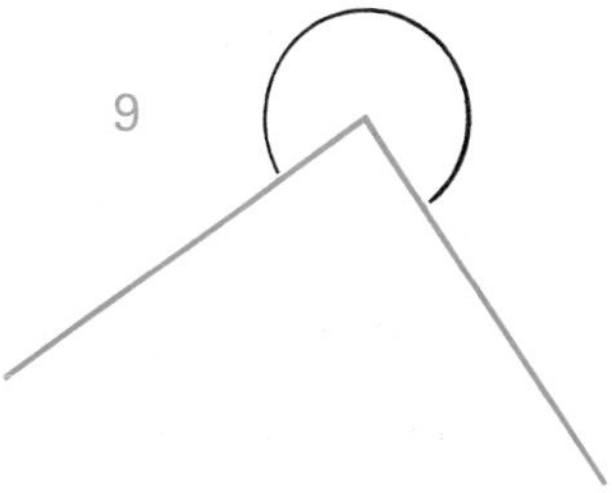

# Measuring angles.

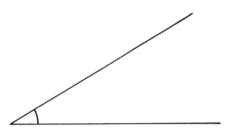

Trace this angle and cut it out of thin card.
This is your unit angle.
Make five more angles exactly the same size.

Use your unit angles to measure these angles.
The first one has been done for you.

1
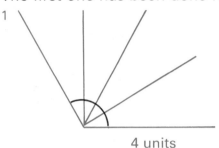
4 units

2

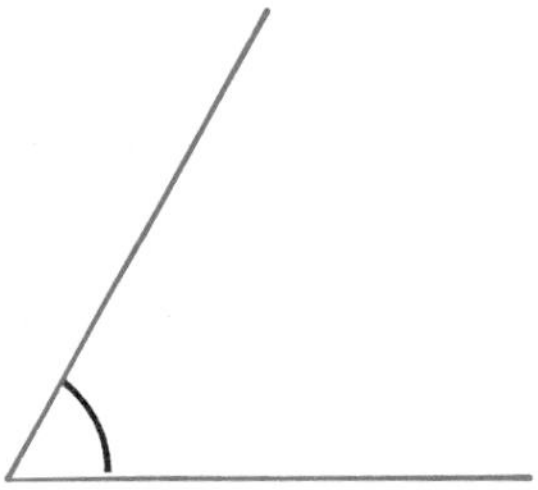

3

4

5

6

Use your unit angles to estimate these angles.

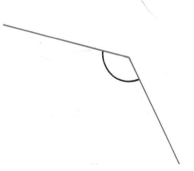

1   Continue the patterns.

   (a)   58, 60, 62, .... , .... , .... , 70, .... , .... , .... , 78

   (b)   110, 107, 104, ...... , .... , 95, .... , .... , .... , ....

   (c)   302, 307, ...... , ...... , 322, ...... , ...... , ...... , ......

   (d)   220, 213, ...... , ...... , ...... , 185, ...... , ...... , ...... , ......

   (e)   171, 163, ...... , 147, ...... , ...... , ...... , ...... , ...... , ......

2   In these patterns the difference between
one number and the next changes in a regular way.
Continue the patterns.

   (a)   3, 4, 6, 9, 13, .... , .... , .... , .... , ....

   (b)   146, 145, 143, 140, ...... , ...... , ...... , ......

   (c)   9, 14, 20, 27, .... , .... , .... , .... , ....

   (d)   100, 91, 83, 76, .... , .... , .... , .... , ....

1003, 7, 29, 94, 236, 12, 7, . . . . . . . .

3   (a)   Monday, Thursday, Sunday, Wednesday, ............ , ............

   (b)   Tuesday, Saturday, Wednesday, Sunday, ............ , ............

   (c)   January, April, July, ............ , ............ , ............ , ............

   (d)   July, November, March, ............ , ............ , ............ , ............

1, 2, 3, 4 ..... ?

5, 4, 3, 2 .... ?

10, 20, 30 .... ?

2, 4, 6, 8 .. ?

4   Here is a trick question,
It may not look like a number
pattern, but it *is*.

   O, T, T, F, F, S, S, .... , .... , ....

5   Make up some number patterns
of your own.
Give them to a friend to complete.
You complete your friend's patterns.

# A hundred square.

This is a column.
↓

| 1 | 2 | 3 | 4 | 5 | 6 | 7 | 8 | 9 | 10 |
|---|---|---|---|---|---|---|---|---|---|
| 11 | 12 | 13 | 14 | 15 | 16 | 17 | 18 | 19 | 20 |
| 21 | 22 | 23 | 24 | 25 | 26 | 27 | 28 | 29 | 30 |
| 31 | 32 | 33 | 34 | 35 | 36 | 37 | 38 | 39 | 40 |
| 41 | 42 | 43 | 44 | 45 | 46 | 47 | 48 | 49 | 50 |
| 51 | 52 | 53 | 54 | 55 | 56 | 57 | 58 | 59 | 60 |
| 61 | 62 | 63 | 64 | 65 | 66 | 67 | 68 | 69 | 70 |
| 71 | 72 | 73 | 74 | 75 | 76 | 77 | 78 | 79 | 80 |
| 81 | 82 | 83 | 84 | 85 | 86 | 87 | 88 | 89 | 90 |
| 91 | 92 | 93 | 94 | 95 | 96 | 97 | 98 | 99 | 100 |

← This is a row.

1  8, 18, 28, 38, 48, ___, ___, ___

   (a)  What are the three missing numbers?

   (b)  What do you notice about all the numbers?

2  Look at the units digit in each column.
   What do you notice?

3  Look at the tens digit in each column.
   What do you notice?

4  Put a counter on each of these numbers on the hundred square:
   10, 19, 28, 37, 46, 55, 64 and 73.

   (a) What numbers do you think the next two counters should go on?

   (b) What number do you get if you subtract each number covered by
       a counter from the next one covered by a counter? Start with 10.

   (c) Start with 8. Add 9 and put your counter on 17 (8 + 9 = 17).
       Continue to add 9 and put a counter on each number you get.
       Stop at 71.
       Which pattern do the counters make:

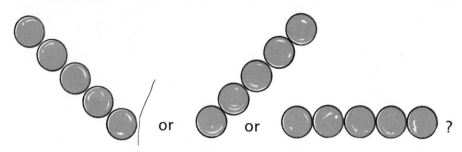

or        or        ?

5  Start with 26. Look at the number below it, 36.
   You add 10 to 26 to make 36.
   Check that the number below is 10 more for all of these:

   (a) 19   (b) 72   (c) 35   (d) 3   (e) 86   (f) 40   (g) 65.

6  Look at 54. The number on its left is 53, which is 1 less than 54.
   Check that the number on the left is 1 less for all of these:

   (a) 15   (b) 28   (c) 37   (d) 49   (e) 54   (f) 60   (g) 82.

7  Start at 53. Go down to the number below it, 63,
   then 1 place to its left, 62.
   You added 10 then subtracted 1.   10 − 1 = 9.

   | 53 |
   | 62←63 |

   Check that other numbers arranged like this
   all have a difference of 9.

8  What do you notice about numbers arranged like this      ?
   Find a reason for your answer.

9  Use squared paper to make a hundred square.
   Mark all the even numbers in blue and all the odd numbers in red.
   What do you notice about the patterns?

10  Make up some number patterns of your own in the hundred square.

## Roman numbers.

The Romans used letters to write numbers.

Here are the symbols they used for
the numbers 1 to 10.

| 1 | 2 | 3 | 4 | 5 | 6 | 7 | 8 | 9 | 10 |
|---|---|---|---|---|---|---|---|---|---|
| I | II | III | IV | V | VI | VII | VIII | IX | X |

Here are some more symbols that were used
by the Romans.

| 50 | 100 | 500 | 1000 |
|---|---|---|---|
| L | C | D | M |

The Romans did not use a place-value system.
They wrote the symbols side by side and usually added the values.

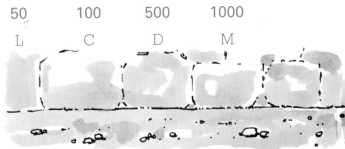

1 + 1 + 1
III = 3
XV = 15
XXV = 25

5 + 1 + 1
VII = 7
XVIII = 18
XXVI = 26

The Romans had two special rules.

A

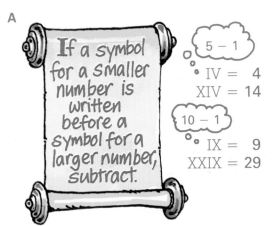

If a symbol
for a smaller
number is
written
before a
symbol for a
larger number,
subtract.

5 – 1
IV = 4
XIV = 14

10 – 1
IX = 9
XXIX = 29

B

Do not write
any one
symbol more
than three
times.

40 is written as XL
(50 – 10)
not as XXXX.

## Write in our number system.

| | | | | | | | | | |
|---|---|---|---|---|---|---|---|---|---|
| 1 | II | 2 | V | 3 | VIII | 4 | XVI | 5 | XIX |
| 6 | XXXV | 7 | XXIII | 8 | LXI | 9 | LIX | 10 | XLV |
| 11 | LXVII | 12 | CX | 13 | CLXV | 14 | CCL | 15 | DC |
| 16 | CDL | 17 | CDLXXV | 18 | DCXLI | 19 | MIX | 20 | MCCV |

## Write in Roman numbers.

| | | | | | | | | | |
|---|---|---|---|---|---|---|---|---|---|
| 21 | 9 | 22 | 14 | 23 | 18 | 24 | 46 | 25 | 58 |
| 26 | 73 | 27 | 91 | 28 | 140 | 29 | 282 | 30 | 356 |
| 31 | 450 | 32 | 527 | 33 | 802 | 34 | 920 | 35 | 1017 |

## Write in our number system the dates of these famous inventions.

**36** Magnetic Compass

MC

**37** Adding Machine

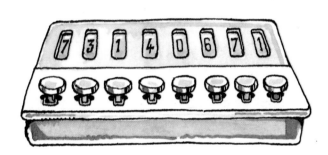

MDCXLII

**38** Motor Car

MDCCCLXXXVII

**39** Safety Match

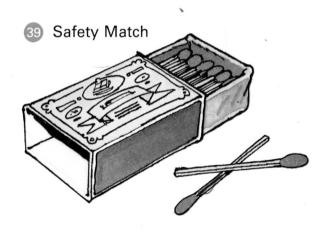

MDCCCXLIV

**ready or not?**

Multiply.

| | | | | | | | | | |
|---|---|---|---|---|---|---|---|---|---|
| 1 | 8<br>×4 | 2 | 7<br>×7 | 3 | 9<br>×7 | 4 | 7<br>×6 | 5 | 8<br>×9 |
| 6 | 9<br>×6 | 7 | 9<br>×8 | 8 | 6<br>×8 | 9 | 4<br>×9 | 10 | 6<br>×10 |

## Multiplying by ten.

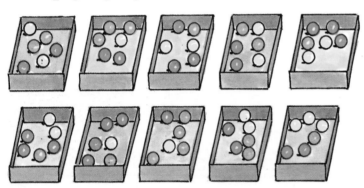

There are 6 marbles
in each box.

To find the total number of
marbles, you can multiply.

```
    6
  ×10
   60
```

Multiplying by 10
is easy.

```
    9        12        18        25
  ×10      ×10       ×10       ×10
   90      120       180       250
```

Do you see an easy way to
multiply a number by 10?

Multiply.

| | | | | | | | | | |
|---|---|---|---|---|---|---|---|---|---|
| 11 | 13<br>×10 | 12 | 15<br>×10 | 13 | 19<br>×10 | 14 | 22<br>×10 | 15 | 26<br>×10 |
| 16 | 34<br>×10 | 17 | 53<br>×10 | 18 | 58<br>×10 | 19 | 62<br>×10 | 20 | 92<br>×10 |

| 21 | 124<br>× 10 | 22 | 156<br>× 10 | 23 | 132<br>× 10 | 24 | 175<br>× 10 | 25 | 190<br>× 10 |
|---|---|---|---|---|---|---|---|---|---|

| 26 | 210<br>× 10 | 27 | 234<br>× 10 | 28 | 353<br>× 10 | 29 | 482<br>× 10 | 30 | 526<br>× 10 |
|---|---|---|---|---|---|---|---|---|---|

| 31 | 672<br>× 10 | 32 | 684<br>× 10 | 33 | 792<br>× 10 | 34 | 800<br>× 10 | 35 | 943<br>× 10 |
|---|---|---|---|---|---|---|---|---|---|

Copy and complete.

36   5  are worth ___ pence.

37   16  are worth ___ pence.

38   23  are worth ___ pence.

39   36  are worth ___ pence.

Solve.

40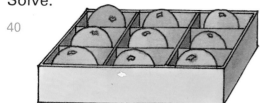

How many oranges in
10 boxes?

41

How many apples in
10 trays?

42   Joe puts 10 pictures on each page
of his photograph album.
How many pictures can he put on
36 pages?

43   June has 43 pieces of straight track
for her electric train. Each piece is
10 cm long. How long is the longest
straight track she can build?

44   You need a calculator. Enter 8 and multiply it by 10. Note that the 8 moves
one place to the left. See if the digits move one place to the left when you
multiply (a) 27 by 10 and (b) 134 by 10.

45   Use the calculator to check the answers to questions 21 to 35.
Do the digits move one place to the left each time?

Sometimes you don't have enough facts to solve a problem.
At other times you have more facts than you really need.

Remember these steps to help you solve problems:

A   Read the problem and find the question.

B   What are the facts?

C   Decide what to do.

D   Answer the question.

E   Does your answer seem right?

What else do you need to know?

1   Kevin earned £1.25 an hour for raking leaves. How much did he earn altogether?

2   Louise found some new buttons she wanted for her coat.
There were 5 buttons on a card.
How many cards did she need?

3   Jeff bought a record. He gave the shopkeeper a £5 note. How much change did he receive?

4   Trevor returned 143 bottles.
How much did he get for the bottles?

5   Sharon's class sold 126 raffle tickets one week.
How many tickets did they sell during both weeks?

6   One hundred and eighty pupils were going on a field trip.
How many buses did they need?

Solve.

7   There were 2000 raffle tickets to
    be sold for the school fête.
    Eighty-four children each
    sold 10 tickets.
    How many tickets were left to sell?

8   Billy watched television for the
    same time each day.
    In one week, Billy watched a
    total time of 630 minutes. How
    many minutes did he watch
    each day?

9   Lucy filled a 42 page album with
    photos. She put 10 photos on
    each page. How many photos did
    the album hold?

10  Fred bought a record for £5.79
    and a book for £1.95.
    He gave the shopkeeper £10.00.
    How much change did he get?

11  Debbie rode her bicycle on a
    50 kilometre tour. During the first
    3 hours she rode at a speed of
    12 kilometres per hour. How much
    further did she have to ride?

12  A pet shop was selling birds at
    £1.50 each. Kate bought 3, and
    then she bought a cage for £5.
    How much did she spend
    altogether?

13  Julie had £16.58. She worked for 3 hours and earned £2.75 an hour.
    How much did she have altogether?

## keeping skills sharp

Calculate the perimeter and the area.

1

2

**Tenths.**

How many squares have been coloured?

 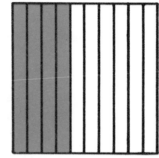

$1\frac{4}{10}$ squares have been coloured.

We can write the number in a place-value table like this:

| Units | tenths |
|-------|--------|
| 1 | 4 |

or without a table like this: 1.4

Such a number is called
a **decimal fraction**
or just a **decimal**.
The dot is a decimal point.
Read "1.4" as "one point four".

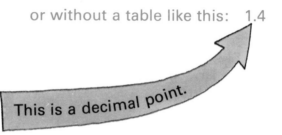

This is a decimal point.

**How many squares are coloured?**
**Give answers as decimals.**

1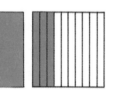

2

3

4

5

6

Give a decimal for the number of coloured squares.

7

8

9

10

11

12

Match.

13  **2.1**    14  **1.2**    ➤

15  **3.2**    16  **2.3**

a   two and three tenths      b   three and two tenths

c   two and one tenth         d   one and two tenths

Write these as mixed numbers with tenths (a) in figures and (b) in words.
Example: 14.2 = $14\frac{2}{10}$   Fourteen and two tenths.

17  **3.6**       18  **4.8**       19  **2.9**       20  **5.0**       21  **6.8**

22  **5.9**       23  **10.3**      24  **15.4**      25  **18.6**      26  **21.8**

Write a decimal that is between the two numbers.
Example: 4, 5  4.2 is between 4 and 5.

27  **3, 4**       28  **5, 6**       29  **9, 10**      30  **18, 19**     31  **21, 22**

32  **14, 15**     33  **25, 26**     34  **28, 29**     35  **1, 2**       36  **17, 18**

# Comparing decimals.

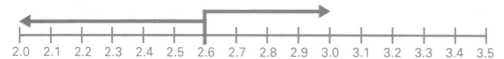

We can see from the number line that
2.6 is nearer to 3.0 than to 2.0.

We say that 2.6 becomes 3 when it is
**rounded to the nearest whole number.**

The numbers on the line increase from left to right.
We can see that 3.1 is greater than 2.9 because it
is further to the right.                    $3.1 > 2.9$          $2.9 < 3.1$

1   **Copy and complete the number line.**

| | | | | | | | | | |
|---|---|---|---|---|---|---|---|---|---|
6.0    6.1    6.2                                                6.8            7.0

**Use the number line to round these following numbers to the
nearest whole number.**

(a)   6.3        (b)   6.9        (c)   6.4        (d)   6.7        (e)   6.6

2

**What is the value at**

(a)   A?        (b)   B?        (c)   C?        (d)   D?

3   **Copy and complete by writing > or <.**

(a)   14.1 ___ 3.9                    (b)   0.6 ___ 1.2

(c)   6.5 ___ 5.6                     (d)   10.2 ___ 9.9

(e)   70.6 ___ 71.0                   (f)   79.9 ___ 88.8

4   **Round to the nearest whole number.**

(a)   36.2        (b)   41.7        (c)   38.3        (d)   72.9        (e)   49.8

# Adding and subtracting decimals.

## Adding decimals

You can find the sum of two decimals
by adding in columns, just as you
did with whole numbers.

```
  1.9
+ 1.7
  3.6
  1
```

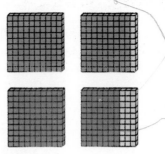

*Note*  The 16 strips are each $\frac{1}{10}$ or 0.1
10 of them equal 1 whole.

## Add

| 1 | 2.6<br>+ 3.1 | 2 | 5.3<br>+ 2.5 | 3 | 0.2<br>+ 0.4 | 4 | 1.6<br>+ 5.2 | 5 | 3.0<br>+ 4.9 |
|---|---|---|---|---|---|---|---|---|---|
| 6 | 0.4<br>+ 0.8 | 7 | 0.6<br>+ 0.9 | 8 | 1.5<br>+ 1.7 | 9 | 0.5<br>+ 2.8 | 10 | 0.7<br>+ 2.7 |

## Solve

11   A garden path was 7.8 metres long.
     It was made 2.9 metres longer.
     How long was it then?

12   Sandra drove 19.7 kilometres before
     lunch and 13.6 kilometres after lunch.
     How far did she drive altogether?

## Copy and complete

13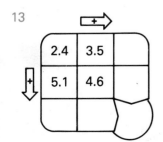

14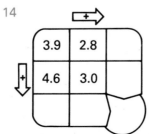

15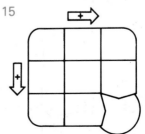

## Subtracting decimals.

You can subtract two decimals
by subtracting in columns just
as you did with whole numbers.
Remember to put the decimal
points one above the other.

$$\begin{array}{r} 2.6 \\ -\ 1.9 \\ \hline 0.7 \end{array}$$

Change 1 whole into 10 lengths.
Then subtract 9 tenths (0.9)
from the 16 tenths (1.6).
Then subtract the whole
number (1 − 1 = 0).

### Subtract

| 1 | 4.7 − 2.2 | 2 | 7.9 − 5.6 | 3 | 3.8 − 0.1 | 4 | 4.5 − 2.5 | 5 | 1.8 − 0.7 |
|---|---|---|---|---|---|---|---|---|---|
| 6 | 5.2 − 3.8 | 7 | 6.3 − 2.6 | 8 | 8.0 − 1.2 | 9 | 7.1 − 4.3 | 10 | 5.7 − 2.9 |
| 11 | 10.6 − 3.6 | 12 | 12.1 − 5.8 | 13 | 23.3 − 11.7 | 14 | 42.0 − 20.2 | 15 | 67.2 − 49.6 |

16 A runner took 58.6 seconds to run one lap
and 60.1 seconds to run the next lap.
Find the differences in the times.

17 Andy decided to walk to his friend's house
which was 4.3 kilometres away.
He stopped for a rest after walking
1.8 kilometres.
How far was he from his friend's house?

18 Sandra weighs 43.7 kilograms and
Bill weighs 46.2 kilograms.
Find the difference in their weights.

# More about adding and subtracting decimals.

To subtract 2.8 from 5 we must write a 0 in the tenths position.

Subtract 2.8 from 5.

$$\begin{array}{r} \overset{4}{\cancel{5}}.\overset{1}{0} \\ -2.8 \\ \hline 2.2 \end{array}$$

If you round to the nearest whole number you can get an estimate of the answer. This helps you to avoid mistakes.

$$\begin{array}{r} 14.2 \\ +83.9 \\ \hline \end{array}$$

Rounding to the nearest whole number we get

$$\begin{array}{r} 14 \\ +84 \\ \hline \end{array}$$

Our estimate is   98

The exact answer is 98.1.

---

1  Rewrite so one decimal point is under the other, then subtract.

(a)  4 − 2.3     (b)  17 − 8.6     (c)  10 − 4.1     (d)  13 − 0.6

(e)  6.2 − 4     (f)  9.1 − 7     (g)  15.6 − 12     (h)  20.3 − 17

2  Round to the nearest whole number and get your estimated answer. Then do the addition.

(a)  $\begin{array}{r} 26.7 \\ +19.2 \\ \hline \end{array}$     (b)  $\begin{array}{r} 53.4 \\ +26.8 \\ \hline \end{array}$     (c)  $\begin{array}{r} 38.9 \\ +\ 5.9 \\ \hline \end{array}$     (d)  $\begin{array}{r} 79.8 \\ +12.3 \\ \hline \end{array}$

3  Round to the nearest whole number and get your estimated answer. Then do the subtraction.

(a)  $\begin{array}{r} 41.1 \\ -16.8 \\ \hline \end{array}$     (b)  $\begin{array}{r} 50.2 \\ -14.6 \\ \hline \end{array}$     (c)  $\begin{array}{r} 49.5 \\ -19.9 \\ \hline \end{array}$     (d)  $\begin{array}{r} 22.0 \\ -\ 9.7 \\ \hline \end{array}$

---

**A decimal game.**

Play this game with one or more friends.
The winner is the player who makes the greatest total.

A  Prepare two sets of ten cards with a different digit on each
   (0, 1, 2, 3, 4, 5, 6, 7, 8, 9).
   Mix up the 20 cards and spread them out, **face down**.

B  Choose a leader.

C  Each player draws this

$$\square . \square$$
$$+ \ \square . \square$$
_____

. is the decimal point.

D  Without looking, the leader picks a card.
   Each player writes the digit in any box.

E  Repeat D until all four boxes are filled.

F  Add. The player with the greatest total scores 1 point.

G  Repeat the game several times. The player with the most points
   is the winner. (Choose a new leader for each game.)

You can vary the game in many ways.
Try these variations:

Play as above but the player with the **smallest** total scores 1 point
**or**
change the + sign to −.

The winner is the player with the **greatest difference**
**or**
the winner is the player with the **smallest difference**.

**keeping skills sharp**

State whether each angle is a right angle, acute angle,
obtuse angle or reflex angle.

1     2     3     4

1  Length/distance.

   (a) A skirt needs 3.5 m of material.
      Mo bought 4.1 m.
      How much material is left
      after making the skirt?

   (b) A car travelled 36.9 km,
      then a further 78.8 km.
      What was the total distance
      travelled?

2  Weight.
Mrs Barnes bought 1.8 kg of beef
and 2.4 kg of lamb.
What total weight of meat
did she buy?

3  Temperature.
Normal body temperature is
37.0 °C. Karl is ill and has a
temperature of 39.9 °C. How much
above normal is his temperature?

4  Volume/capacity.

   (a) A bottle can hold 83.7 cm$^3$
      when full. It has 55.9 cm$^3$ of
      scent in it. How much more
      scent is needed to fill the bottle?

   (b) A car uses 12.7 litres of petrol
      one day and 8.9 litres the
      next day. What is the total
      amount of petrol used?

5  Speed.
A cyclist won a race at a speed of 34.7 km per hour.
The cyclist that came second was riding at 33.8 km per hour.
Find the difference between the two speeds.

# Using a table.

Claire and her father went to see a motor race.
The results of the race can be found in the table.

| Driver | Time, in minutes | Speed, in km per hour |
|--------|------------------|-----------------------|
| ADAMS | 54.0 | 222.0 |
| BENDER | 54.8 | 218.7 |
| DAVIS | 53.9 | 222.3 |
| GARCIA | 54.2 | 221.3 |
| PRIDE | 55.6 | 215.8 |
| ROGERS | 54.6 | 219.5 |
| THOMAS | 54.3 | 221.1 |
| WEAVER | 54.4 | 220.4 |

1  Draw a blank table as shown at the top of page 61. Write in the names of the drivers in order of the time they took, fastest first. (Don't fill in the last column yet.) Who was the winner?

2  What was the speed of the car in fourth place?

3  How much longer did the third car take than the winner?

| Place | Driver | Time, in minutes | Speed, in km per hour | Speed, to nearest km per hour |
|-------|--------|------------------|-----------------------|-------------------------------|
| 1 |  |  |  |  |
| 2 |  |  |  |  |
| 3 |  |  |  |  |
| 4 |  |  |  |  |
| 5 |  |  |  |  |
| 6 |  |  |  |  |
| 7 |  |  |  |  |
| 8 |  |  |  |  |

4 Which drivers were:
(a) faster than Garcia?
(b) slower than Garcia?

5 How many minutes more did the last car take to finish the race than the winning car?

6 What was the difference between the speeds of the first and last cars?

7 How many minutes behind the winning car was Adams?

8 Which driver drove at 1.8 km per hour slower than Garcia?

9 Which driver took 0.4 minutes longer than Adams?

10 Round the speed of each driver to the nearest whole km per hour. Write your answer in the table you drew for question 1.

Reading scales.

A

B

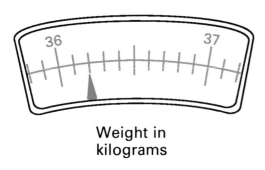

Weight in kilograms

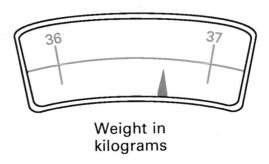

Weight in kilograms

Each division in A is $\frac{1}{10}$ or 0.1.
The arrow is pointing to 36.2 kg.

There are no marks on the scale between 36 and 37. We can estimate the reading is about 36.7 kg.

In the following questions write the readings on scale A and on scale B.

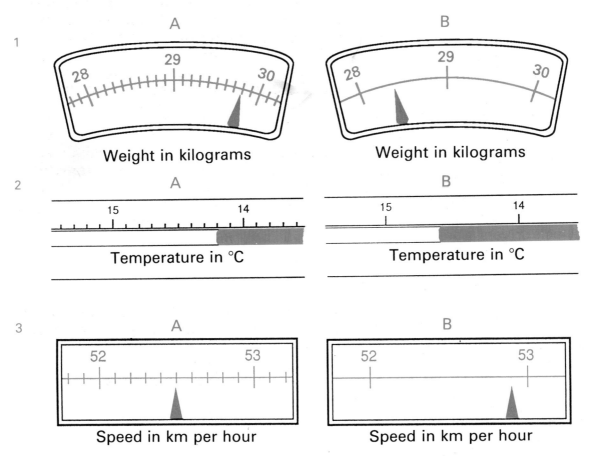

1

A                                    B

Weight in kilograms              Weight in kilograms

2        A                              B

Temperature in °C                Temperature in °C

3        A                              B

Speed in km per hour            Speed in km per hour

There are 100 °C between freezing point (0 °C) and the boiling point of water (100 °C). °C is read as "degrees Celsius".
Check with your teacher to make sure you have the right sort of thermometer for each of the activities.

1  Put the thermometer in a glass of cold water.
Estimate what the reading will be after 2 minutes.
Record: (a) your estimate;
         (b) the reading after 2 minutes;
         (c) the difference between (a) and (b).

2 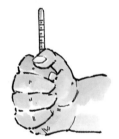 Hold the thermometer in your hand for 2 minutes.
Cover the 'bulb' with your hand as in the picture.
Estimate what the reading will be after 2 minutes.
Record: (a) your estimate;
         (b) the reading after 2 minutes;
         (c) the difference between (a) and (b).

3  Put the thermometer in hot water for 2 minutes.
Estimate what the reading will be after 2 minutes.
Record: (a) your estimate;
         (b) the reading after 2 minutes;
         (c) the difference between (a) and (b).

4 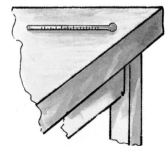 Put the thermometer on a table or desk for 2 minutes.
Estimate what the reading will be after 2 minutes.
Record: (a) your estimate;
         (b) the reading after 2 minutes;
         (c) the difference between (a) and (b).

## Temperature.

The temperatures below were taken at 8 o'clock in the morning, one day in February.

London 5.4 °C        Washington (U.S.A.) −2.1 °C        Moscow −5.6 °C

Berlin 3.2 °C        Rome 8.7 °C                              Paris 4.5 °C

1

L has been written on the number line to show the temperature in London.
Copy the number line on to graph paper.
Mark the temperatures on your line, using the first letter for each city, W, M, B, R and P.

2   Draw a block graph to show the temperatures.

3   What is the difference in temperatures between

(a)   London and Washington?        (b)   Moscow and Rome?

(c)   Paris and Berlin?              (d)   Washington and Moscow?

4   If the temperature rose by 4.8 °C what would the temperature then be in

(a)   London?        (b)   Washington?        (c)   Moscow?

(d)   Berlin?        (e)   Rome?              (f)   Paris?

5   If the temperatures dropped by 5 °C what would the temperature be in

(a)   London?        (b)   Washington?        (c)   Moscow?

(d)   Berlin?        (e)   Rome?              (f)   Paris?

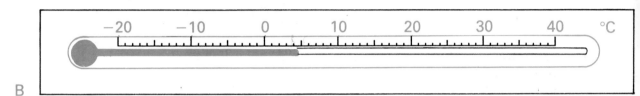

A

This is a clinical thermometer.
It is used when taking a person's temperature.
The normal temperature is 37.0 °C.
The temperature shown on the above thermometer is 37.8 °C.

| −20 | −10 | 0 | 10 | 20 | 30 | 40 | °C |

B

The temperature shown is a little over 4 °C.
We cannot read thermometer B accurately
to the nearest 0.1 °C.
We could estimate it though.
If we had a magnifying glass
it might look like this:

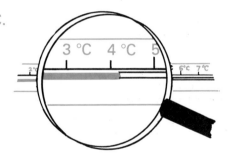

The estimated temperature is 4.2 °C.

1   Using the thermometer A above find the following differences
    in temperature.

(a)  37.4 °C and 38.1 °C       (b)  40.3 °C and 39.6 °C

(c)  33.9 °C and 40.0 °C       (d)  38.2 °C and 37.2 °C

2   Using the thermometer B above find the following differences
    in temperature.

(a)  12 °C and 18 °C       (b)  5 °C and −6 °C       (c)  −2 °C and −1 °C

(d)  3.7 °C and 5.1 °C     (e)  7.0 °C and −2.6 °C   (f)  −1.8 °C and −3.4 °C

3   Find the new temperature if these temperatures rise 1.8 °C:

(a)  36.9 °C       (b)  37.3 °C       (c)  40.8 °C       (d)  0.3 °C

(e)  −3.6 °C       (f)  −0.7 °C       (g)  −10.0 °C      (h)  −1.8 °C

| No chance | Poor chance | Even chance | Good chance | Certain |

For each question your answer is to be one of these:
No chance. Poor chance. Even chance. Good chance. Certain.

1  If I toss a coin it will be a 'head'.

2  I will be alive in the year 2200.

3  If I take one card from a pack it will be an ace.

4  I will be married before I am 30 years old.

5  I will become a teacher.

6  Next Christmas Day will be on December 25th.

7  I will marry a man.

8  The next person to leave this classroom will be a girl.

# Probability.

You need ten cards like these:

| 0 | 1 | 2 | 3 | 4 | 5 | 6 | 7 | 8 | 9 |

Give your answers as:

No chance. Poor chance. Even chance. Good chance. Certain.

1   Sally is blindfolded.
    She has taken two of the cards.

    What is the chance that

    (a)   the total of the two numbers is 19?

    (b)   the total of the two numbers is 1?

    (c)   the difference between the two numbers is 1?

    (d)   the difference between the two numbers is 8?

2   Use the ten cards. Mix them. Put them face downwards.
    Turn over the top two cards. Write down the total.
    Repeat this 30 times. Record your results in a tally chart
    like the one below.

**Sally's tally chart showing total of 2 cards**

|           | 1 | 2 | 3 | 4 | 5 | 6 | 7 | 8 | 9 | 10 | 11 | 12 | 13 | 14 | 15 | 16 | 17 |
|-----------|---|---|---|---|---|---|---|---|---|----|----|----|----|----|----|----|----|
|           | I |   | II |   | IIII | II | III | II | IIII | III | II | I | I | I | II | II | I |
| Frequency | 1 | 0 | 2 | 0 | 3 | 2 | 3 | 2 | 4 | 3 | 2 | 1 | 1 | 1 | 2 | 2 | 1 |

3   There is **No chance** of the total for two cards being 0, 18 or any
    number greater than 18.
    For all the numbers from 1 to 17 say which of these apply to the
    total if you select any two cards:

    No chance. Poor chance. Even chance. Good chance. Certain.

You have to choose between four answers, A, B, C or D

For example: Without counting, estimate the number of dots in the circle.

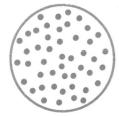

A  210        B  47        C  78        D  110

The correct answer is B.

1   How many dots are there in this rectangle?

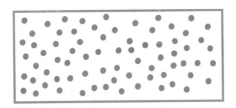

A  105        B  134        C  56        D  73

2   What is the greatest distance from the sea of any place
    in Great Britain?

    A  205 km        B  60 km        C  120 km        D  300 km

3   How tall is a full grown oak tree?

    A  120 m    B  2 m    C  20 m    D  50 m

## keeping skills sharp

| 1 | 6.7 <br> + 3.8 | 2 | 9.2 <br> + 7.9 | 3 | 4.6 <br> + 24.6 | 4 | 18.4 <br> + 7.5 | 5 | 36.5 <br> + 18.7 |
|---|---|---|---|---|---|---|---|---|---|
| 6 | 3.9 <br> − 1.7 | 7 | 9.0 <br> − 6.2 | 8 | 7.4 <br> − 3.8 | 9 | 16.1 <br> − 8.4 | 10 | 20.4 <br> − 13.7 |

First estimate, then find the answer by counting or measuring.

1   How long would it take you to count up to 1000?

2   Part of a lawn is a square with sides 1 metre. How many blades of grass are there in the square?

   Hint:  If you count the blades of grass in a square with sides of 10 cm, you can multiply this by 100 to get your answer for a metre square.

3   How many postage stamps could you fit on to the top of this mathematics book?

4   1 kg = 1000 g = 20 × 50 g.

Use the information above to find the number of sweets (any kind you like) that weigh 1 kg.

   Hint:  Weigh 50 g of sweets.
            Count them and multiply by 20.

5   How much does the water in a cup weigh?

   Hint:  Weigh the cup and the water, then weigh the empty cup and find the difference.

6   (a)   Use a method like the one in question 4 to find the number of new pencils needed to weigh 1 kg.

   (b)   What is the weight of one pencil in grams?

   Hint:  Use a calculator to divide your answer to (a) into 1000. This will give you the weight of one pencil in grams.

7   How much does 1 sheet of paper weigh?

   Hint:  Weigh 100 sheets, then use a calculator to divide the answer by 100.

1. What is the greatest 4-digit number you can make if no digit is used twice?

2. There are many ways of making 12 using two numbers.
Here are some: $6 + 6$, $14 - 2$, $6 \times 2$, $100 - 88$.
Find some more.

3. John was looking at an old calendar.
April 14th was on a Saturday.
Give the dates of all the Tuesdays in that month.

4. Using all three of the digits 7, 3 and 2 you can make six different 3-digit numbers.
Find them all.

5. You can only use the numbers 7 and 2, also $+$ and $-$.
Make all the numbers 1, 2, 3, 4, 5, 6, 7, 8, 9 and 10.
For example, $7 - 2 + 7 - 2 = 10$.

6. $\square + \bigcirc + \triangle$

   Use 0, 1, 2, 3, 4, 5, 6, 7 and 8.
   Put one number in each of the three shapes to make 8.

   Examples: $\boxed{5} + \bigcirc{2} + \triangle{1}$, $\boxed{2} + \bigcirc{5} + \triangle{1}$,

   You can only use a number once each time.
   Find as many ways of making 8 as you can.

7. Ask a friend to think of a number, but not to tell you what it is.
Tell your friend to: add 3; multiply by 3; subtract 1;
subtract the number he or she started with;
divide by 2; subtract the number he or she started with again.
The answer will be 4.
Try it with other friends. The answer will always be 4.

8. How old am I?
Last year my age could be divided exactly by 7.
This year it can be divided exactly by 5.
I am not yet 48 years old.

1    845
    + 97
    ————

2    6327
    +2844
    ————

3    There are 1284 pupils in one school
    and 1768 pupils in another school.
    How many pupils are there altogether?

4    Add    216 + 69 + 382 + 556

5    £8.37          6    471          7    702
    + £6.94            − 235             − 386
    ——————            ————             ————

8    323 − (109 − 42)

9   This shape has been
    built with cubes.
    How many cubes were
    needed to build it?

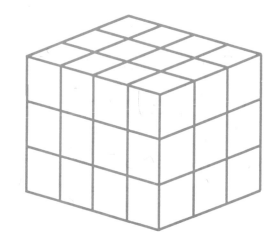

10  Draw a rectangle.
    Mark all the right angles
    like this

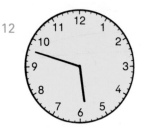

11  Complete.
    A cube has ___ vertices

                ___ edges

                ___ faces.

12   Write the time in two ways.

    (a) ____ minutes to ____

    (b) ____ : ____

13  Ann said she would meet Joe at 18:52.
    She was 20 minutes late.
    At what time did she arrive?

14  Ed had £20.
    He spent £11.85.
    How much did he have left?

15  Tina bought a scarf costing £14.80
    and some gloves costing £8.95.

    (a)  How much did she spend?

    (b)  How much would she have left out of £80?

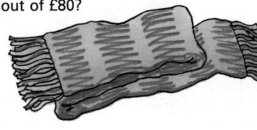

16  (a)  8 × ____ = 48

    (b)  ____ ÷ 7 = 8

    (c)  5 × 9 = ____

17  There are 9 chairs in each row.

    (a)  How many chairs in 4 rows?

    (b)  There are 72 chairs.
         How many rows are there?

18  (a)  (4 × 6) + 23 = ____

    (b)  90 − (63 ÷ 9) = ____

19  Write down any three multiples of 6.

20  Write down a common multiple of 4 and 5.

21  (a)  5 × ____ = 40

    (b)  ____ × 10 = 70

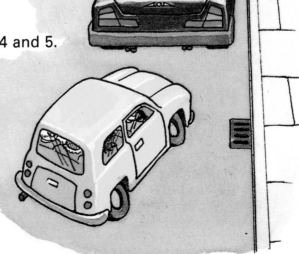

22  30 people went to the theatre.
    There were 5 people in each car.
    How many cars were needed?

23 Karen and Ted want to buy some furniture costing £371.70.
They have £236.90.
How much more money do they need?

24  represents 25 eggs.
What do these represent?

25 (a) $27 \div 9 + 18 =$

    (b) $3 \times (32 \div 4) =$

26 What fraction is shaded?

27 $\frac{1}{3}$ of 21 =

28 $\frac{1}{2}$ of a number is 18.
What is the number?

29 Gary spent $\frac{1}{3}$ of the £12 he had.

    (a) How much did he spend?

    (b) How much did he have left?

30 Complete the instructions
so that a rectangle is
drawn.

FORWARD 35   RIGHT 90
FORWARD 15   RIGHT 90
FORWARD ___   _____ ___

_____ ___ _____ ___

31  Draw all the lines
    of symmetry.

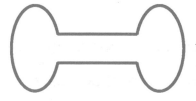

32  (a)  **32 × 3 =**

    (b)  **18 children. How many toes?**

33  (a)      76
           **×  2**
           ———

    (b)      87
           **×  4**
           ———

34  Multiply £0.37 by 8.
    Give your answer in pounds.

35  Find the total cost of 12 pencils costing 8p each
    and 23 pens costing 9p each.

36
    2)‾6‾8‾

37
    6)‾9‾6‾

38  Complete          2   R
                   4)‾9‾7‾
                    − 8
                    ———
                     17
                    − 16
                    ———

39  Divide 91 by 5.

40    Measure the sides.
    Their lengths are _____ , _____ , _____ .
    The perimeter is _____ .

41  Draw a rectangle 3 cm long
    and 2 cm wide.
    Find the area.

    Area =

42  List the prime numbers
    between 15 and 24.

43  Find the volume of the cuboid
    if the edges of the small cubes
    are 1 cm long.

    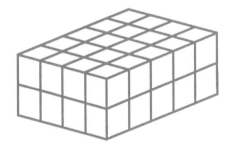

44  (a)  3 litres = ____ millilitres.

    (b)  What is the weight in grams
         of 63 millilitres of water?

45  Complete this tally chart.

| Tallies | Frequency |
|---|---|
| ЖЖ ЖЖ III | |
| | 9 |
| ЖЖ ЖЖ ЖЖ I | |

46  How many days are there from March 20th to April 9th?

47  There are 16 cakes. Ed ate $\frac{1}{4}$ of them and Gary ate 6.
    How many were left?

48  Draw   (a)  an acute angle

       (b)  an obtuse angle

49  Complete this number pattern.

    112, 105, 98, _____ , _____ , _____ , _____ .

50  (a)  Write MCCIX in our number system.
    (b)  Write 91 as a Roman number.

51  46 × 10 =

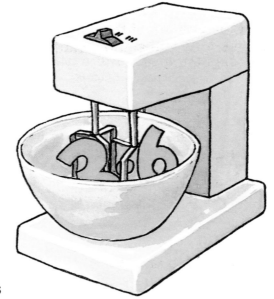

52  Write 3.6 as a mixed number.

53     32.3
     − 19.8
     _____

54  Two pieces of string have lengths
    28.2 cm and 17.5 cm.

    Find   (a)  the sum of their lengths
       (b)  the difference of their lengths

55 A tank holds 43.7 litres of petrol when full.
It has 19.8 litres in it.
How many more litres are needed to fill the tank?

56 What weight is shown?

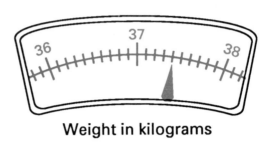

Weight in kilograms

57 The temperature rose from 11.2 °C to 14.0 °C.
What is the rise in temperature?

58 The temperature in Moscow was 4.8 °C.
During the night it dropped to −1.4 °C.
How may degrees did the temperature drop?

59 If 5 coins are tossed there will be 4 heads and 1 tail.
Choose the correct answer.

| No chance | Poor chance | Even chance | Good chance | Certain |
|-----------|-------------|-------------|-------------|---------|

60 Estimate the number of dots in the circle.
Choose the correct answer, A, B, C or D.

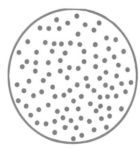

A  225        B  100

C   71        D  192